# CHOOSING **HEALTH**

# CHOOSING
# HEALTH
## INTENTIONALLY

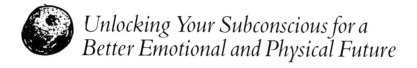 *Unlocking Your Subconscious for a Better Emotional and Physical Future*

## XANDRIA WILLIAMS
### WITH MICHAEL MORTON-EVANS

Published in the UK in 1992 by
Charles Letts & Co Ltd,
Letts of London House,
Parkgate Road,
London SW11 4NQ

First published in Australasia in 1990 by
Simon & Schuster Australia,
7 Grosvenor Place, Brookvale,
NSW 2100

A CIP catalogue record for this book is available from the British Library

'Letts' is a registered trademark of Charles Letts & Co Limited

Printed in the United Kingdom

# PREFACE

This book is first and foremost about *choice*. You can choose to act on the information contained herein, or you can choose to ignore it. You can choose the bits of it that suit you and your lifestyle, and choose to ignore the bits that don't. Whatever you decide to do, the decision is yours and yours alone — and that, in a nutshell, is the message contained in this book.

We, the authors, choose to believe that, by taking complete responsibility for our own lives we are empowered to alter the course of those lives, for better or for worse. Of course, there are those who will say that our lives are preordained and that nothing we do will affect the ultimate course of them, and there will be those who are convinced that disease and illness are the results of outside agencies and that we have little or no control over them. For them, too, this book is about choice — their choice of belief.

There is considerable evidence that our thoughts and emotions can affect the state of our bodies. We all know, for example, that worry can sometimes cause headaches or ulcers. We know that fear can sometimes cause the digestive system to play up, resulting in nausea or diarrhoea. There is also a growing body of scientific evidence, coming from both medical doctors and physicists, that the power of our thinking and our attitude (a result of the direction of our thoughts) can influence our lives and the world around us.

We suggest, therefore, that the information presented in this book is, at the very least, worth considering. It may severely strain your belief in parts, but remember that what you believe is largely a result of the way in which you were raised and trained. What if your parents and teachers were wrong? Now may be the time to start rethinking some of your long-held beliefs. The choice is yours.

There are various intelligent, well-trained people around the world who think that persuading people to believe that they alone have caused the illnesses they suffer from is burdening them with an unfair measure of guilt, and that, since it can never be categorically proved one way or the other, this blame only leads to further unnecessary suffering. Let us say, here and now, that if you read the book throughout you will find that there is absolutely no suggestion that anyone should feel guilty for causing their condition, but rather that they should congratulate themselves for finding a safe and socially acceptable way of dealing with the fears, needs, uncertainties, and so on, which they encounter in their lives.

We cannot know yet with absolute certainty whether or not the thesis presented in this book is true, but we cannot, likewise, say with absolute certainty that it is *not* true. So consider which of the two possibilities is the more helpful to you at this point in time. If, like us, you feel that it is more helpful to believe that you do have control of your present physical and emotional health you will find the many useful tips for a better life contained in the book of great benefit to you. On the other hand, you may prefer to believe that your life is like a cork bobbing on the ocean of uncertainty and gain little from the information within.

The choice is yours.

# CONTENTS

# INTRODUCTION

The aim of this book is to help you untangle, harness and use the mental and emotional energies which are inside you. Free from mental, emotional and physical problems you can lead a happier, more fulfilled life.

None of us is a victim of bad health. We are, however, influenced by the system of beliefs which, consciously or unconsciously, rule our lives. Our personal belief systems have been built up from even before we were born, and certainly much of the groundwork was laid and reinforced during our childhood. If, for example, your family was one that expressed emotion then you are likely to be comfortable doing that; but if your family believed in a 'grin and bear it' attitude to life and to health, then you are sure to operate under the same principles of stoic acceptance.

The thing is that *every* aspect of our lives is determined by the belief systems that have been constructed since our birth. We unconsciously choose to continue operating within them — whether it is good for us or not. But we can *choose* to change. We can *choose* good health. We can choose to understand how our health is linked to our emotions, which in turn are linked to our conscious and unconscious thoughts, the direction of which are influenced by our belief systems. This is what *Choosing Health Intentionally* is all about.

So how do you choose? What it necessitates, of course, is a clear understanding of yourself — why you act and think the way you do. Many people think they know themselves, and so they do — up to a point. But most people rarely look below the surface and certainly never make the connection that the past can deeply influence our present and future.

This capacity to choose a better direction is not only of extreme importance to the individual but, of course, has wider ramifications. We are not separate entities existing alone: we are part of a society and world population with which we have far-reaching links and connections in all sorts of ways. Certainly we can choose to make things better for ourselves, but surely that choice will also somehow affect those other individuals to whom we are connected, and then, like a ripple on a pond, outwards to still others?

We think that the world is a place upon which we can have no influence or control. It can be a frightening place where it seems that no matter what laws are passed in the parliaments of the world, we cannot ensure that one day some madman somewhere isn't going to push the button that will set off the greatest conflagration in history. If that prospect seems too extreme and unlikely, there are the daily news reports of man's inhumanity to man. There are wars in Ireland and the Middle East, for example, or the treatment of black South Africans by whites, or, for that matter, the treatment of black Australians.

And if we are not intent on destroying each other, then we seem to be determined to destroy the environment in which we live. Continual assaults on the ecosystem are destined to make it so unstable that it must in the end disintegrate, while species continue to become extinct at an alarming rate. We jeopardise our food supplies, our water supplies and even the air we breathe. Our daily use of fluorocarbons is slowly destroying the ozone layer, creating a greenhouse effect which will gradually melt the polar icecaps, raise sea levels and cause world-wide flooding. Our use of various dangerous pollutants, encouraged by profit-hungry multinationals and ignored by careless governments, adds to the long list of ways man-kind has devised to destroy itself.

When a single person contemplates these problems they can seem so vast that the only safe place to put your head seems to be firmly in the sand. After all, what point is there in picking up one piece of rubbish from the pavement when all around you people are throwing it down by the tonne?

Believe it or not, there *is* something you can do. If you take a leaf out of the book of the *Macaca fuscata*, a breed of monkey which lives in Japan, there is a more than even chance that you, whoever you may be, can be instrumental in saving the whole world from destruction.

One particular colony of the *Macaca fuscata* living on the island of Koshima, was the subject of a thirty-year study by scientists and during the period of observation an extraordinary change of behaviour pattern was discovered. These monkeys normally eat a variety of buds, fruits, leaves, shoots and the bark of over 100 types of plants. Their pattern of eating had been taught to them by their mothers, who, in turn, had learnt from their mothers before them.

As part of an experiment, the scientists started giving the monkeys raw sweet potatoes covered with sand to eat, a situation that was completely alien to the monkeys. For some time the animals were perplexed by the situation until, one day in 1952, a young female, who had been christened Imo by the scientists, hit on a solution to the problem. She took her potato to a nearby stream and began washing the sand off it. Imo then taught this trick to her mother, reversing the age-old pattern of instruction, and then taught her playmates, who, in turn, taught it to their families. Slowly the number of monkeys washing their sweet potatoes began to grow, until 1958 when the pattern suddenly changed and there was a startling explosion in the number of monkeys using the technique.

The most extraordinary and important element of this event was that monkeys all over mainland Japan and even on the outlying islands inexplicably began washing their food at the same time. It was as though some unseen force had relayed this piece of good news across the country to be picked up by the entire monkey population.

It was an event for which the scientists were totally unprepared and for which they had no explanation. However it prompted author Lyall Watson in his book, *Lifetide*, to suggest that there may be an evolutionary mechanism other than natural selection, and that by this mechanism changes can be spread throughout the community once a certain critical mass has been achieved. The Hundredth Monkey Effect, as it has become known, gives us all hope, for it was just one monkey on her own who began the whole process.

If one young monkey can change the eating patterns of every monkey in a whole country, why can't one human being be responsible for a change in the behaviour pattern of the world? If every one of us sets out to develop our own emotional health and well-being and to assist those around us in this goal, then ultimately a great web of positive energy will be created which must surely have a profound effect on the negative and destructive habits of mankind. With this in mind no-one should feel that their individual effort is too puny or too worthless. It is, rather, a vital part of building the Hundredth Monkey Effect.

But it still comes down to the individual — and the individual's choice to make a positive change in him or herself. You have to understand yourself and, when you have done that, you have to want to make changes.

Exploring and really getting to know yourself can seem strange, even frightening at times. It's not something most of us are particularly practised in — when do we have time for a start? A good (and fun!) way to begin your voyage of self-discovery is to try and work out what temperament you have.

The four basic temperaments of mankind — choleric, sanguine, phlegmatic and melancholic — were first acknowledged in mediaeval physiology and are still used today as the basis for accepted psychological tests such as the Eysenck Personality Inventory, devised by the British psychologist Hans Eysenck. Almost everyone is a mixture of all four temperaments, but generally people have one which dominates the others. They can be used to provide an insight into a person's emotions and personal and social relationships.

Each of the temperaments can in turn be divided into three stages of development in the manner described by Danish psychologist, Knud Lundt in his book, *Understanding Our Fellow Man*. The first stage is the immature and egotistical, followed by the maturing and experienced stage and lastly one reaches the fully mature stage where, theoretically at least, you should have a clearer outlook on things, having fully developed the best attributes of your temperament. In reality the stages will overlap to some degree and you can oscillate between them depending on circumstances and outside stimuli. Chronological age has little to do with your stage of development. You could be a mature stage three choleric even in your teens, or an immature stage one phlegmatic in your fifties. It all depends on your own growth and development.

So the first step in getting to know yourself is to establish which is your dominant temperament. Having perhaps surprised yourself in that directon, it is useful then to recognise the way the other temperaments combining within you contribute to your personality, and then to learn to recognise the temperaments in other people so you can start to understand and respond to them accordingly.

## CHOLERIC

Cholerics are quick-witted extroverts who are conscious of their own worth and quick to take the lead. They dislike weakness of any kind. Leadership, courage and endurance are the keys to their temperaments but they have to learn to listen to others and keep their temper.

First-stage cholerics can be tyrannical and insist on their own way. They hate being told what to do and hate being criticised. By the time they reach the second stage, however, cholerics have learned to listen to those they can respect and have learned to distinguish false praise; they can be moved by genuine sorrow and have developed a kind and chivalrous heart. To reach the third stage is difficult, but if successful the choleric will have learned to control his temper and be more tolerant; by the third stage cholerics become adored and encouraging parent figures.

## MELANCHOLIC

It's usually fairly easy to pick a melancholic — not only do they feel depressed and gloomy, but they look it, too. Everything about them droops — their clothes, their shoulders, their heads.

First-stage melancholics demand pity and seek sympathy and understanding all the time. Progress to the second stage, however, finds them wavering between egotism and self-denial. They would prefer to be unselfish but have insufficient strength to maintain their resolve. But melancholics who develop through to the third stage learn that their greatest satisfaction is being of value to others.

They learn to find great enjoyment in working with people who are suffering either physically or emotionally.

## PHLEGMATIC

A well-balanced, orderly, not over-exciting life is what the phlegmatic craves. They weigh everything up carefully and are not keen on new ideas. Phlegmatics are not leaders but, being co-operative and reliable, will do their best to carry out instructions.

First-stage phlegmatics can show great attention to detail but without guidance or supervision can be utter failures. With the right leadership, however, they will move on to stage two and will be your friend for life. Only in this stage will they start to consider anything new and only then very cautiously. By stage three phlegmatics undergo a huge change. They will, by hard work, have reached a position of trust. They are still pretty solid and unadventurous, but are deadly efficient, completely honest and hardworking.

## SANGUINE

Sanguines are extroverted, optimistic and cheerful, and can develop a real Peter Pan image both physically and mentally. They are quick and clever which, because they hate repetition and boredom, can lead to a reputation for being a dilettante. They are liable to drop projects as quickly as they pick them up.

There can be a blurred line at times between first-stage sanguines and cholerics for both like to be the centre of things. The difference is that the choleric will lead you on to glory whereas the sanguine is liable to drop you in a mess when things become tough. In the second stage sanguines are full of good intentions but often lack the strength of character to accomplish them. They need a hero to emulate to help develop their own maturity and sense of self-worth. Should sanguines progress to the third stage they reach a lovable and generous state. They share their optimism, are passionately interested in anything new and have finally developed the ability to complete or delegate what they start.

These then are the four temperaments of mankind. Which one do you think you slot into? It is an interesting first exercise in self-analysis, just to get you started. Don't worry if you find that you don't fit neatly into any one of the four. There will be bits of each in you as there are in all of us. They show up in varying proportions depending on the circumstances in your life. But try to determine your predominant temperament, for to know that is to start knowing yourself.

# UNDERSTANDING THOUGHT

Our human view of life is generally as restricted as that of a flea living on an elephant. Our knowledge is limited by our experience and we tend to equate things with our known surroundings, making judgments based on our limited knowledge and awareness. Like the flea who has spent its life living on the hindquarters of an elephant, we have no experience of the trunk or the tusks, or the over-all vastness of our host. If, however, the flea were to be shaken off its perch and land on the grass, it would be amazed, in looking around, to see the elephant. For the first time it would be able to put the whole animal into context and would immediately gain a better perspective of its former home.

Likewise, humankind, having been limited in its knowledge of the planet earth, suddenly began to form a whole new picture when Neil Armstrong landed on the moon, and pictures of our planet were beamed back from outer space. For the first time we could really begin to put ourselves into perspective against the rest of the universe. The trouble is that, although it fascinates us, the universe is so vast we are overwhelmed by its magnitude, so most of us prefer not to think about it. Thus we revert to the narrow outlook of the flea on the elephant.

Despite the fact that we tend to shy away from the unknown, we still find ourselves confronted by certain imponderable questions. One of the biggest of these, which has confronted humankind from the start, is the question of creation. Who or what created us? Who or what created Earth? And our solar system? Our galaxy? All the other galaxies? In fact, who or what created the universe?

It is fair to say that nobody knows the answers with absolute certainty. We do know, however, that the universe is made up of matter and that matter is, in the long run, at the quantum (or subatomic) level, the same as energy. Albert Einstein's famous equation, $E = mc^2$, in his theory of relativity, shows this relationship between energy (E) and mass (or matter) (M). At the most fundamental level they are equivalent. The conversion of matter to energy and vice versa is a constant occurrence. Conversion of matter to energy takes place during such diverse events as nuclear fission reactions and the conversion of food to body heat, while an example of energy into matter can be seen in atomic fusion and the growth of plants from water, carbon dioxide and the sun's energy (and so, ultimately, the growth of humans!). Matter and energy are different forms of the same thing. So consequently there must be a constant level of underlying energy (a kind of cosmic energy) that is being continually reformed into matter and back again.

If everything can be converted to energy at the most basic level, it is perhaps not unreasonable to assume that thought is also a form of energy. If you can imagine that thought waves are like radio waves then you will understand that a thought does not simply end, nor its energy disappear, once it has been thought, or even once the action that is its outcome has been performed. Instead you can imagine thought waves travelling out from a transmitter (the individual) in every direction and continuing on and on into the infinite distance. However, unlike radio waves, unconverted thought waves are not as easily picked up. As an ever present form of human energy it would be wonderful if we could learn to tap into it, rather like the sharing of body warmth generated when people huddle together.

To make another heating analogy, could we not use our thought energy to alter a particular situation just as heat will warm a saucepan of cold water? By using thought energy we could alter the outcome of events in our lives, either directly, like the heat applied directly to the saucepan, or by what we say or do, forming a chain reaction like nuclear fission.

What does this idea of thought as energy have to do with our health? Back in the 1930s scientist and medical practitioner Alexis Carrel wrote in his book, *Man, The Unknown*: 'The mind is hidden within the living matter [and remember that matter is energy at its most fundamental level]...completely neglected by physiologists and economists...almost unnoticed by physicians. Yet it is the most colossal power of this world... Each state of consciousness probably has a corresponding organic expression [that is, a physical manifestation]... Thought can generate organic lesions...' Although it may seem a radical idea that your thoughts can create your state of health or ill-health, the idea has been around for quite a while, and is backed up by many eminent scientists and philosophers.

The idea that thought is energy pouring out like waves or forming complex chain reactions would also seem to suggest that there is a huge, ever-flowing web of thought in which the energy is converted into action or is translated into different forms of energy, such as emotions.

We could perhaps look upon this great thought-energy collection as a form of Universal Intelligence, of which all our thoughts are a part and into which we could tap. It would be an orderly formation because, as Einstein pointed out, the universe is orderly and runs along predictable and consistent lines.

This concept of universal thought and/or intelligence is not just fantasy. It has not only been accepted by great scientific minds in the West but is part of the ancient philosophies of the East. Encapsulating these theories, let's consider the following possibility:

> If thought makes up intelligence, and if thought is energy and each thought forms part of a great universal web of energy, then all intelligence is a single unity. All thought is one thought and all laws are one law.

If this is indeed the case, then you are tapping into the universal thought every time you think and thus your mind is part of the universal mind. Do you think that's mad? Then think about the air you are breathing. Now take a deep breath and hold it in your lungs for as long as you can. While you've got it there, try to answer the following questions:

> Is the air in your lungs your air?
> Is it someone else's air?
> Is it universal air?
> Where has it been?
> Has it come from someone else's lungs?
> How clean were they?

Now breathe out and ask yourself where the air is going. Will someone else now breathe in that particular air? Given that thought is even less tangible than air, is it not possible that it can be shared in exactly the same way?

People have a wide variety of names for this Universal Intelligence. It has been called God, Allah, Buddha, Prana, the Lifeforce, the Collective Unconscious and Chi, to name but a few. Call it what you will, most people recognise it in one form or another.

As members of the human species we are born with certain sensory limitations. We cannot see as far as the eagle, hear as well as the bat or smell as keenly as the deer. In spite of this we tend to believe that if we cannot detect something it doesn't exist, though as we know, this is not the case. We are also bound by cultural and religious limitations that are placed on us depending on which strata or race of the species we are born into. Behaviour and beliefs which are readily accepted in some cultures are not quite believed or accepted in others. For example, it is quite all right for a man in Saudi Arabia to have six wives, but such behaviour would earn you a lengthy jail sentence in Sydney or New York.

Finally, each individual sets his or her own limits based partly on personal experience and partly on upbringing. Any unhappy experience in one situation can quickly lead to a generalisation of that unhappiness to cover all similar experiences. For example, because a holiday in Bali resulted in a bad attack of gastric upset, all Asian destinations are viewed with grave suspicion or even shunned completely. Because an early love affair ended unhappily, all contact with the opposite sex may be shunned and considered dangerous and undesirable. Thus the average human being is beset by limitations on all sides and, influenced by these limitations, we each create our own view of the world.

In doing so we may create a view that is totally unlike that of the next person. If the disparity is small, as is generally the case, no comment may be made and we may feel that we are indeed in touch with reality and our truths are universal truths. However, if the disparity is large, we are liable to be branded by our society as eccentric, unreliable or even mad. We are not, they say, in touch with reality.

But what is reality? In a general sense, reality is what the majority of people in a particular community believe in and feel safe with. Anything outside this norm is viewed with about as much suspicion as stone-age cave dwellers would view a lawnmower. What we now have to do is unfetter ourselves from some of these self-imposed limitations and start to explore new frontiers, allowing others to explore these uncharted areas at the same time, without the risk of being branded as loonies or dismissed as irresponsible 'alternative' drop-outs.

This brings us to another major question. Given the limitations surrounding us, or even given that we can throw them off, to what extent do we actually control our lives? Do we have any control over our lives at all? Or is it all in the hands of fate? Is there any point in planning our lives or has it all been pre-planned for us so that we might as well just sit back and take whatever hand we are dealt?

You might believe in fate without even quite realising it. Fate comes in a number of shapes and sizes and the most popular of these is called 'God'. God (or whatever name or names you choose to use) was invented almost the minute homo sapiens had the power of thought in order to explain away all the things that man couldn't find answers for. It became a very convenient excuse for a whole range of behaviours. Some of the worst atrocities the world has witnessed have been done in the name of one god or another, simply because it was more convenient to have someone else to blame rather than take responsibility oneself. The ancient Greeks and Romans for example had a whole panoply of gods, one for every aspect of life, and when life didn't come up to their expectations they reasoned that it was because the appropriate gods were angry with them. The Incas of South America were good at that reasoning too, as were the Egyptians. In fact humankind as a whole, faced with impossible questions, collectively looked for someone else to blame and an unexplainable external power was the obvious answer. Of course, God (or the gods) did good things, too, according to this way of thinking, but people were somewhat slower to acknowledge that, preferring to take the credit for themselves.

As man gradually began to find more and more answers for the imponderables surrounding him, he has been able to take more responsibility for his actions. Nevertheless, there are still a great many unanswered questions and God is still a useful way for people to cope with them.

So what do you believe? Do you believe wholly in some outside controlling force? Do you believe that you control your own destiny? Or do you hedge your bets and believe a little each way, whenever it suits the occasion?

If you believe that you do *not* control your life, then surely you have to accept that anything you do, anything you achieve, is in the hands of the external power and could be wiped out at any minute. With no power over your own life, you might as well suppose that there is little point in trying to accomplish anything that requires any effort because you will fail if your controller has not pre-ordained success. Anything that happens to you is going to happen anyway, because that is what your controller has planned. Any thoughts that you have hardly matter since your entire future has already been mapped out for you; you might as well just wake up each morning and see what 'God' has organised for you that day. The power of thought is rendered impotent because no matter how much you dislike your situation you will believe that you can't escape. In short, why bother at all?

The fence sitters will believe that when things are going well they are in control, but when things go bad, something other than themselves must have been responsible (rather like the ancient Greeks and Romans!). Or in a version that leans more towards individual control, the fence sitter will believe that events are thrown up by God and then the individual has a choice in how to deal with them. Those who believe this will argue that there is a greater pattern to their lives and that each experience can be used to learn from, or is the opportunity to take a new branch on their personal road through life.

There are also those who believe that they have full control over their lives. This is not to say that they do not necessarily believe in some external creative force (although sceptics also fall into this category), but they do believe that they can create their own life paths. If you think this way, then surely there is some point in creating things the way you want them? There is some point in striving towards a goal, some point in planning for the months and years ahead, some point in developing your own philosophy of life. For most of us it seems a far safer bet to lead a life over which we are fully in control, than to wonder from one day to the next if life ('God') is going to let us down. Of course, being in control of anything or anyone brings its own responsibilities and these can be quite daunting.

We may never know for sure what the truth of this matter is. This being the case, let's consider which version is the more useful. Clearly it is more *useful* to believe that we are in control over our lives than that we are in the helpless grip of fate. At least then we can take control of our lives and head for positive outcomes rather than lie back in a sea of helplessness.

Let's go back to the basic element of this discussion — our thoughts. Our thoughts can be considered to be active within us at two levels. There are the thoughts of which we are conscious and which, to a large extent, we can control. There are also those thoughts that make up our subconscious, all those buried memories and ideas which are built up from our past experiences and decisions, and which make up the backdrop of our lives. It is these subconscious thoughts that dictate and filter the way we see the world today, as well as the way we behave in it. The subconscious provides many of the limiting factors that we mentioned earlier. Surprisingly, few of us are aware of the basis of this subconscious and fewer still can reach into it, learn about it or analyse it. It frequently takes an outside jolt (perhaps this book or one of our Choosing Health Intentionally workshops) to enable you to recognise the effect the workings of the subconscious are having on your life.

Just as electricity (another form of energy) can be blocked or channelled in a particular way to create certain effects, so too can our thought energy (both conscious and subconscious) be blocked or channelled — sometimes in ways inappropriate for our health and well-being. Once we learn to understand *why* we have limited or channelled our thought energy in a particular way, we can go about directing it in the way that is most beneficial to us and our lives.

When you decide to explore this past and subconscious programming, you will find you can change your life and create it the way you would like it to be in the future. It's entirely up to you. The limiting factor at this point in your life is only yourself.

C H A P T E R    2
# THOUGHT IS CREATIVE

Thought is one of the most powerful tools that we have in our possession. The simple thought of one person can be responsible for changing the whole pattern of the world. Like a bush-fire which can start from a tiny spark and destroy a thousand square miles of forest, a tiny thought can blossom into an earth-shattering conclusion. So we should try to harness and direct this energy. Remember, positive thinking on the conscious level can nearly always produce positive results.

How often have you slung your leg over the edge of the bed in the morning, feeling really rotten, and said to yourself 'Today is going to be a rotten day'. And sure enough it has been a stinker! Or alternatively you may have leapt out of bed, flung back the curtains, listened to the birds singing and said 'Wow, today's going to be great'. And sure enough it is!

If you go for a job interview believing that you are going to get the job, you are far more likely to succeed than if you enter the room convinced you don't stand a chance. People who have convinced themselves that they are going to succeed exude a compelling air of confidence which is bound to give them the edge over the slightly sheepish, hang-dog appearance of their less confident rivals.

Positive thought is like a long chain made up of links. Art Gresham, an American sociologist from Manhattan, ran a non-scientific test in New York in 1969 to see if it was possible to change people's moods in the early morning. One of the things he did was to choose a typical bad-tempered New York cab driver on whom to test his theory. Climbing into the taxi he asked to be taken downtown and, after the usual hair-raising ride at high speeds, he alighted at the other end, paid the driver and, smiling, said 'Thank you, that was a most pleasant ride. May I say you drove beautifully.' The driver's face broke into a smile. At that moment a woman carrying a mound of parcels shouted at the cabbie. To the sociologist's amazement the driver got out of his cab, something no cab driver in New York ever does, helped the woman pile her parcels into the back seat, held the door open for her while she got in, and drove off. The simple act of praising the driver had started a chain reaction which he felt sure would be passed on right through the day. The woman would get out of the cab, thank the driver, feel good about what had happened and say something equally nice to the doorman of her block of apartments. He in turn would smile at the postman and have a kind word for him, the postman would start to whistle and feel better than he had done all day and so it would go on. Over a period of some days, using this technique, Gresham followed people and satisfied himself that he was, in the majority of cases, correct. So you see, one small action, initiated by a single thought, can start a whole reaction that can change people's lives.

If you are a sporting fan you will know that at least 80 per cent of a sportsman's winning ability lies in his mental attitude on the day. If he is psyched up to win he will do far better than if he approaches the match on a downer. Twenty per cent of his winning ability lies in his skill as a sportsman, but it is that other 80 per cent, the mental attitude, which will win him the match. Determination plays a great part in winning. Determination is what gets mountaineers to the top of the highest peaks and marathon runners to stay the distance. But what is determination? Nothing more than another name for positive thinking.

The course of your life can be altered simply by the way you think and feel. Your thoughts have the power to make things happen. Do you remember the time you were thinking of your mother and that you hadn't heard from her for ages, and then she suddenly phoned? Or remember the time you thought how nice it would be to have a gin and tonic but you hadn't got any gin, when all of a sudden a friend turned up with a bottle? Coincidence is the name that we give to events which seem to happen without conscious direction, yet we may well have made them happen by the power of our own minds. If you start to believe in the power of thought, then the coincidence ceases to be a chance happening and becomes a positively created event through an attitude of mind. Everything that happens to you is created by you and for some reason. Since we have the ability to direct our thoughts to form positive outcomes, it would seem appropriate to develop skills so that our abilities are of maximum benefit to us. There are a number of different ways in which you can do this. One of the most pleasurable, and most effective, is called creative visualisation. This is simply a means of using your imagination to create a picture in your mind of anything that you might want in your life. Then, having created the picture, you continue to focus on it regularly, thereby giving it positive energy until, in the end, you achieve what it is you have been visualising.

Say, for example, you are having trouble at work with

your boss, but you like your job and don't want to quit. Here's what you do. First, get yourself into a completely relaxed state, perhaps in a room away from traffic and family noise. A little soothing music playing quietly in the background will help too. When you are settled begin to imagine you and your boss together. You are having a conversation. He is praising you for something you have done. He is smiling and friendly and you feel warm towards him. You thank him for his kind words and shake his hand. The two of you continue to talk. It is a pleasant, relaxed conversation and you are both smiling and laughing. It is obvious that you are getting on very well together. You like each other. Now that you have created that picture, try to feel within yourself that what you have just seen is indeed possible. Try to feel that it is already happening, that it is already a fact.

Repeat this procedure two or three times a day, or more if you have the time, being careful of course not to do it when you should be working and thereby giving your boss actual cause to sling off at you! If you do this visualisation regularly and you genuinely want the change to come about, you will soon find that your relationship with your boss is improving. Finally the problem will disappear completely.

But, we hear you say, that's all very well as far as you are concerned, but what about my boss? How is it going to work if he/she isn't doing it too? Well the answer is it will. It will because once your new attitude towards your relationship begins to be reflected in your approach, your boss will have to re-evaluate his/her relationship with you and their approach to you will start to change as well. A great number of the problems we encounter in life are created by our initial approach to the subject. Change your tactics and the problem changes as well.

Like most other things in life you have to believe in

this technique for it to work effectively. And like every-thing else, practice makes perfect. The more you use crea-tive visualisation in your life the more effective you will find that it becomes.

It may all seem a bit strange and far-fetched to you at first, but so was electricity when it was first presented to people. Now we just take it for granted, not necessarily because we understand it, but because we know that it works and is always there. So it is with creative visualis-ation. It is not necessary to understand why it works, just that it does and after a while you can take that for granted as well.

The best person to start on is yourself, especially if you are still feeling a bit unsure about these ideas. We will do a creative visualisation which will help put you in touch with some of your emotional blocks. To do this you will first have to tape record the instructions that you will be giving yourself because there are too many to remember. When you are ready you can settle down in a quiet darkened room, sit back in a comfy chair, close your eyes and play the tape. This is what you should hear your voice telling you (record it slowly, with long pauses so that your mind has time to perform the instructions):

> Imagine that you are blind — you have always been blind. So has everyone else. You have learnt about your environment by your other senses:
> Your sense of touch — imagine yourself feeling your way around.
> Your sense of hearing — imagine how acute your hearing would become.
> Your sense of smell — imagine how important it would be, for example, if you were making toast!
> Your sense of taste — how much you would rely on it to know what you're eating.

Now, because you have no sight, many words have no meaning for you. Words such as colour, red, blue or green, for example. And words such as shadows, or see, watch, look, light and dark or vision.

Now someone you don't know arrives and tells you that they can *see* what is 100 metres away. They try to describe light and dark to you and what colour is like. They try to cope with your limited vocabulary. Could they really explain it to you? Do you believe them?

If you don't believe them, does this make what they see untrue for you — or them? You have a choice. You can either ignore them and decide that they are lying, or you can accept that what they say could be true, at least for them. In which case you can assume either that it is true for them but impossible for you, or if it's possible for them then it could be possible for you as well.

If it's possible for you too, then you can try to develop the skills for yourself, or at least check them out.

Now let's use creative visualisation in a personal situation:

Think of the person you would like to be. First, concentrate on your looks. Picture yourself the weight you would like to be. If you think you are overweight, imagine how you would look with those extra kilos gone, the trimmer figure, the youthful suppleness. If you would like to gain weight, picture the way you would prefer to see yourself. See yourself erect and healthy. Now concentrate on the details...mentally change your skin, your hair, your nails, in fact any of the details about you which you would like changed. See yourself exactly the way you would like to be.

Next imagine the lifestyle you would like to lead.

See yourself doing all the things you would like to do. Think about the person you would like to be. As you see yourself in this visualisation, imagine behaving in the way you want to behave. If you are ever cross, shy, nervous, late or depressed, and wish you weren't, this is the time to change your behaviour. Do the same with your home and possessions.

As you see yourself changing, look around you at your friends and family. How are they changing as a result of the changes in you? How do you feel about this? Is it what you want? Examine the whole situation thoroughly. Perhaps you are pleased with the result, in which case enjoy it. If you are not, change whatever is necessary to achieve a result with which you *are* happy.

Keep this image in your mind and recall it whenever you choose. Certainly recall it whenever the going gets tough, whenever you are feeling downhearted or dissatisfied. Recall this image of yourself and believe in it. You can bring the changes about if you choose to, and probably a lot more easily than you may have thought.

Let's look at a couple of examples of how this can work. Geraldine had always wanted to travel. She felt that all life's excitement lay somewhere 'over the rainbow' and she hankered for a long time for greener pastures. Yet when she did this visualisation she realised that if she did all the travelling she wanted, she would have to give up the job she loved, and would probably lose touch with a lot of her friends. As a result she realised that what she really wanted was more glamour in her life — and travel had always meant glamour to her. When Geraldine thought about it, she discovered lots of small ways to bring more glamour and excitement into her life without having to travel for it.

David, on the other hand, had always been shy and tongue-tied socially, yet he knew he could get on well with people once he got to know them. He created an image of himself as a socially at ease bachelor about town. Immediately before any social occasion he took ten minutes by himself to recreate this image and then went straight into the fray. Very quickly he found his self-confidence rising and he began to enjoy many of the occasions that had previously disconcerted him.

These then are your first important lessons in creative visualisation. This powerful technique will enable you to harness the power of positive thinking by creating your own visualisations about anything that you want to change in your life. All you have to do is see your life as you would like it to be and believe it to be so. This technique works for literally thousands and thousands of people all over the world. It can work for you.

# CHAPTER 3
# DREDGING YOUR MIND CLEAN

Creative visualisations are an extremely important skill which not only direct the power of positive thinking at a conscious level, but help you to visualise a strong self-image to balance any negative undercurrents and self doubts in your subconscious.

The subconscious, all those hidden thoughts derived from buried memories and conditioning, is very influential. All your daily decisions are made against the backdrop of your subconscious, and if it is filled with negative beliefs, all areas of your life, including your health, will be adversely affected. Negativity is a life-destroying force which we might as well try to eliminate from our daily menu so we can live a physically and spiritually healthy life.

Generally the most devastating negative beliefs, and the ones that can do you the most damage, are the ones you have about yourself. For instance, if you keep telling yourself that you're stupid, then that's how things must be. What's more, being an ingratiating little critter, the subconscious mind thinks it has to do its best to please you, so it sets out to fulfil your expectations and prove you right, largely by guiding you to concentrate on things that will underline your beliefs. It is also your obedient servant and will guide you to do all the things you need to fulfil your expectations as well.

Write down in a list of two columns all the beliefs you have about yourself — positive and negative. Be honest. It's an even bet that the list of negatives is a great deal longer than the list of positives. It's truly amazing the propensity we have for beating ourselves up, yet when it comes to being kind to ourselves we feel almost guilty. We'll come back to these positive beliefs a little later, but as it is what's holding you back that you're trying to change, we'll deal with the negative beliefs now.

Here are some of the negative beliefs which we most commonly hold. Do any of these appear on your list?

## RELATIONSHIPS
Everybody hates me
I cannot express love
My mother/father/husband/wife doesn't love me
Nobody understands me
My father didn't want me
I am jealous of my brother/sister
My colleagues don't like/respect me
When they find out what I'm really like they won't like
   me any more
I am too domineering
Nobody ever pays any attention to what I say

## MONEY AND POSSESSIONS
It's too expensive
I never have enough
Money causes arguments
My self-worth is measured by my income

My possessions are more valuable than my relationships
    with other people
Money is the root of all evil
You have to cheat to be really wealthy

*SELF-IMAGE*
I am too fat/thin
No-one will love me if I go bald
I am getting wrinkles
I am without grace
I am too young/old
I'm too stupid
I don't deserve anything good
I'm not good enough

And so they go on.

Take a close look at your own list and decide which belief seems to be the most important (and the most devastating) in your life. The one you choose is your Primal Negative Belief or PNB. It may be something like 'I am not good enough', or 'I'm too fat'. You may seem to have more than one PNB, in which case write them all down, and again, try to decide which is the most important, the most fundamental.

These primal beliefs are the basic belief patterns that people become stuck on. Consciously or unconsciously they believe these things to be true and their lives are guided by them. Obviously if you have a strong negative belief about yourself you are going to be guided in a direction which is probably not the most advantageous to you. However there are a number of ways in which you can clear up these negative beliefs in processes which can be likened to cleaning the dirt from the bottom of a pond.

Your primal negative belief will be either inert or active. If, for example, your primal belief is 'I am not good enough' (and you would be amazed just how common this one is), in its inert form you would tend to do nothing, believing that, since you aren't good enough, there is little point in trying anything. If your primal belief takes an active form, however, it may manifest itself in a superiority complex. What you are in fact doing is overcompensating for feeling that you aren't good enough.

If you now want to clear up these and similar issues with yourself, there are two ways in which you can effectively do so. They should be used together to form a barrier against your negative belief system and, better still, turn the negatives into positives. To use the analogy of cleaning the pond again, if you imagine that your mind is the pond and you would like the water to be fresh and clear, you first have to dredge up all the muck from the bottom. So go back to your list of negative beliefs about yourself and add any you have about other people, and about events, activities and feelings. Once you have successfully got all this 'dirt' floating about on the top of the pond you can start to scoop it off until the pond is crystal clear.

To use the cleansing mechanism it is first necessary to fix the belief in time and space. Here is a simple procedure: If your most negative thought about yourself is 'I am too fat', complete the statement 'I am too fat because...' If the completion is 'Because I eat too much' then complete the next statement: 'I eat too much because... I feel anxious'. Go on with the process, 'I feel anxious because...' If the completion to that statement is 'Because I am not loved', you have probably hit upon a primal negative belief. Your PNB is that you are not loved or maybe that you are not a lovable person. Do not be sidetracked and do not fool yourself with long and complicated answers. Keep it simple and crystal clear.

Take another example. If your most negative thought

is 'I am not intelligent', then complete the statement 'I am not intelligent because . . .' If the completion is 'Because I do not apply myself', then complete the statement, 'I do not apply myself because . . . I feel I will not succeed.' 'I will not succeed because . . . because I am not good enough.' And there you have arrived at another of the most common PNBs.

Having established your most negative thought about yourself you are now ready to move on to the second part of the process which is the positive alternative — the affirmation. This is a positive statement you make about yourself which you believe to be true.

The human brain, for all its sophisticated and intricate set-up, is remarkably easy to fool. If you tell it something forcibly enough and for long enough it will start to believe it. The easiest way to fool the brain is by doing affirmations.

The purpose of the positive affirmations that we are going to suggest you make is to take your primal negative belief and turn it into a positive one. After all there is little purpose in walking around for the rest of your life in a cloud of negativity when you can just as easily turn these negative aspects of your life into positive ones.

Doing affirmations is the most effective way there is of cleaning up the pond of your subconscious. They are simple and easy to do and need little more than a small notebook, a pencil and, every so often, a few minutes of your time.

Taking the negative belief 'I am not loved', for example, you now write down the affirmation 'I (name) am loved and wanted'. Write it down at the top of the first page in your notebook or on a sheet of paper. Now draw a line down the middle of the page. The space to the right of that line is your Release Valve. This is where you can note down the dismissive responses the little voice in your head is going to make when you write down the affirmation ('I am loved and wanted') in the left-hand column.

Now write down your affirmation 'I, (name), am loved and wanted' 20 times in the left-hand column. If your little voice wants its say, write that down too. (Eventually the little voice will have raised all the objections it can and become bored, in which case you leave the right-hand column empty.) Repeat this process as often during the day as time will allow, and keep it up for a week or two. If your PNB is, say, 'I am not good enough', your positive affirmation could be something like: 'I approve of everything I do', or 'I succeed in everything I do'. It is not good enough simply to turn the words around to create an affirmation. For example, if your PBN is 'I am not good enough', your affirmation should not be just 'I am good enough', that's a cop out. Create a really positive affirmation such as the ones suggested above to counteract your PNB. You will be surprised just how effectively your affirmations will work after a while.

Don't give up halfway through, and don't give in to thoughts that the whole exercise is a waste of time and a load of nonsense. Believe that the process works, allow it time to work, and work it will. Whatever you believed in the past, your attitude and actions helped to make it so. Your future actions, fuelled by a positive belief in yourself, can bring about a new and more desirable future.

Besides your primal negative belief you will have many others, all of which are holding you back and limiting you. Just think of the lists you made earlier. You can use affirmations to learn about and change the whole pattern of your life.

Go back to your list of negative beliefs and put a ring around the one which you now think is worse than all the others, worse in the sense that it is the one which is causing you the most grief *at this moment*.

Let us say your worst belief at the moment is 'I am ugly'. Take that statement and proceed this way:

I am ugly because . . . (complete the statement).
    Let's imagine you've written 'because I dress badly'.
I dress badly because . . . I'm afraid of being called sexy.
I'm afraid of being called sexy because . . . people will
    think I'm a tart.

You have just discovered one of the belief systems which was laid down early in your life. Now is the time to examine it. Does being attractive really mean that you're a tart? Think about this rationally. Think of all the attractive, well-dressed people you know and admire. Are they tarts?

Having located this negative belief, create a positive affirmation to combat it. In this case something like 'I, Mary, am attractive, liked, and people respect me'. Say it to yourself several times and write it down so you can use it later.

Another negative belief might be 'I am always poor' or 'I am a failure'. In processing those beliefs you might come up against the fact that you find money evil, or that you have to cheat to become rich, or that you find success frightening and the responsibility that it may bring too much for you. When you are working on these negative beliefs don't wallow around in long and complicated sentences. Stop. Find something short, sharp and to the point and use it to reprogramme your subconscious. Remember, the truth is simple!

Everyone can have a number of different negative beliefs at different levels. They can change all the time, and you have to try to determine which one is uppermost in your life at this present moment. Having determined it, remember that the bottom line comes back to you and no-one else. It is simply an opinion which *you* have about *yourself*. Often you will assume that others hold this opinion too, but you know what they say about the word assume: it usually makes an 'ass' out of 'u' and 'me'!

Having faced the opinions which you have about yourself, you can now set about changing them for the better. Change your PNBs and the rest of your life will change at the same time. Your responses to people and events will alter proportionately to the shift in your perceptions.

Now let's look at your *positive* beliefs. Go back to your original list of positive and negative beliefs. Is the positive column as detailed as the negative column? Is it as kind to you as your negative list was critical? It's very difficult, isn't it, to say to yourself 'I'm a really clever and likeable person', or 'I am good looking and intelligent', or 'Everyone wants to know me because I am so amusing'. You'd feel kind of big-headed doing that, wouldn't you? What sort of conditioning have we had that makes it okay to believe nasty thoughts about ourselves but deny the nice ones? It's crazy, isn't it?

Many of us were brought up from childhood being conditioned in this way. You might have rushed home from school proudly to show your mother some piece of work you thought was rather good, only to be told that it wasn't nice to boast. Or perhaps you might have been keen to participate in some activity only to be told that it wasn't good to push yourself forward. These and many more little parental warnings helped to mould your thinking as you grew up.

Now's the time to stop squashing yourselves. The cure can be simple. Start saying nice, positive thoughts to yourself however secretly guilty you may feel, and in no time at all your subconscious will begin to believe them and guide you towards an altogether better way of life. If you do nothing else in the way of self-improvement from this point on, try at least to stop beating up your subconscious and enjoy the difference in your life.

Let's finish this chapter with a small visualisation. Close your eyes and imagine a beautiful yacht ploughing through the waters of the ocean. Being pulled along behind the yacht at the end of a long rope is a small dinghy. Fix the helm so that you are on a safe course and go below. Search out all the rubbish on board and pile it into large green garbage bags, tie them up and toss them out on deck.

Be aware that the rubbish is made up of all your unwanted and negative thoughts and emotions. Climb up on deck and pull the dinghy towards you. Start piling the large green plastic bags into the little boat. Keep remembering that the bags are full of all the rubbishy things you have been thinking about yourself and other people. Think of any other negative thoughts you have been entertaining in your mind and put them into garbage bags, too. Then pile all of these extra bags into the dinghy. When the yacht has been completely cleared, cast off the rope and watch as the dinghy floats gently away on the tide. It moves further and further and further away, until it is just a small speck on the horizon. Finally it has disappeared, taking all your rubbish with it. Imagine that you are free at last from all that negativity and can sail briskly through the waves again without any unnecessary ballast. Now slowly open your eyes and feel good about yourself.

C H A P T E R 4
# LEARNING BEFORE YOU WERE BORN

Having mentioned in the previous chapters the negative beliefs formed in the subconcious, and how to air and eliminate them, it is now a good idea to discover how such negative conceptions developed. Understanding ourselves is the key to controlling the health of our bodies. So let's try to go back and understand ourselves — even before we were born.

We mentioned in Chapter 1 that mankind has asked itself questions (such as where do we come from and why are we here?) and tried to find answers for them since time immemorial. Various hypotheses have been ventured, but now, in the twentieth century, as a result of centuries of orthodox religion, orthodox teaching and an overall general conformist attitude among Western peoples, it is usually accepted that life begins in the womb and ends in the grave.

Oriental philosophies, however, hold completely different beliefs which are generally pooh-poohed by Westerners, and if anyone tries to suggest to your average American, Australian or European that we have all actually lived somewhere before and will be reincarnated after death into another body they are likely either to roll around laughing like a demented hyena or rush you off to the nearest insane asylum.

Go on, be honest! Do you believe you have lived somewhere before? And do you really believe that you will live again somewhere else? Most probably not. But just keep an open mind as we develop this subject. Understanding ourselves in order better to control the health of our bodies also involves trying to understand more about the meaning of life. We will never reach any true understanding of that meaning unless we are prepared at least to look seriously at all the possibilities, however daft some of them may at first appear.

Many of the people who have been doing research into this area of life have been extremely distinguished and highly-trained scientists, and some of the results they have come up with have been nothing less than startling. Startling, that is, to those people who were brought up firmly convinced of the cradle to grave cycle.

One such woman is Dr Helen Wambach, a 65-year-old American psychologist, who set out in the mid 1970s to show that we had all been somewhere before we came to this life on this planet. As part of a highly organised experiment with 750 men and women across America, Dr Wambach hypnotised them and asked them a number of questions.[1] The results were, to say the least, unexpected. Of the 750 subjects, 81 per cent said under hypnosis that they chose to be born and that it was their choice to make. Many of these said that they were not alone in making this decision but had the help of an adviser or counsellor. Ninety per cent of the subjects said that death was an enjoyable experience, but strangely a majority of them said they only decided to be reborn reluctantly or after taking advice on the matter.

Even more surprising was the finding that almost all of the 750 subjects, who had been drawn from a cross-section of the American population and had the experience under hypnosis of having chosen to live this life, did not feel that they were part of the foetus until after six months of gestation. Many reported moving in and out of the foetal body right up until the actual birth process. Nearly all of them reported being aware of their mother's emotions before and during birth.

While some of this may seem too far-fetched for words because our upbringing and teaching has been dependant on centuries of being told something quite the opposite, some of it is beginning to fit in neatly with latest research in neurophysiology. While the old Freudian theory was that personality did not start shaping in a child until the second or third year of life, the latest research into the process of the developing foetus indicates that many doctors believe that awareness and consciousness develop in a foetus somewhere between the 28th and 32nd weeks. At this stage the neural circuits are as developed as they will be at birth and the cerebral cortex (that's the brain) is sufficiently developed to be aware of certain things.[2] This certainly makes you stop and think for a moment. Why should we be so dismissive of things that seem strange?

Other scientific studies have shown conclusively that our personality starts to be moulded while we are still in the womb. One such long-term study carried out on adolescents at the Fels Research Institute in Ohio, America, showed that a child's reactions in the womb were translated into later life. As babies they were subjected to loud noises in the womb and their heartbeats were monitored. Those who were not unduly disturbed by the sound were found to be more likely to be placid as an adult later. By finding the womb a safe and pleasant place to be, they developed a trust and confidence which they took with them to the outside world. Conversely those babies whose heartbeat became erratic when exposed to the loud noises displayed highly emotional tendencies as teenagers and were liable to be more introverted and mistrustful of the world at large.[3]

To form personality a human being requires three basic ingredients: emotional capacity, intellectual capacity and neurological capacity. In other words he must be able to feel, think and have the machinery to do so. Obviously the most important of the three is the latter and, as scientific studies have now shown, that all-important prerequisite is present at a very early stage in the baby's development.

The workings of our emotional and intellectual capacities are a process of those parts of the human brain known as the hypothalamus and the autonomic nervous system. A baby's communication with the outside world is made through his mother via the neurohormonal system. Mum transmits the message to the foetus through this system and the baby processes it via the hypothalamus which is the initiator of all emotional states. The hypothalamus will then transmit the necessary signals to the autonomic nervous system and the appropriate action will be taken.

It stands to reason therefore that if a baby in the womb is subjected to high amounts of any particular emotional stress the hypothalamus, which reacts rather like the thermostat on an air-conditioning unit, is going to become 'set' at a certain level. It may be set too high, or conversely it may be set too low. In either case the child's personality is going to be affected in some way. Nobody is quite certain yet at what point a foetus's brain and nervous system are permanently affected by too much of the mother's stress-related neurohormones, nor are we certain exactly what sort of changes these produce in a child, however we do know that every baby is affected by them to varying degrees. Studies that were done with children who had undergone severe stress in the womb have shown that they are more likely to suffer from a whole range of emotional and physical disorders (everything from schizophrenia to milk allergies) than those who have had a relatively stress-free gestation period.

Amazing as it may seem, even though the baby is locked away inside this dark, well-insulated float chamber, he is capable of discerning with remarkable accuracy what is going on outside. During this time different types of brain waves can be detected in the foetus which means that brain activity is underway. And in the last three months before birth the foetus starts to develop a memory. Since everything the brain takes in is remembered and stored somewhere, it stands to reason that somewhere buried within you today are those earliest foetal memories which you formed before birth. Often the key to understanding your personality today lies in unravelling, exploring and releasing those locked-away memories. How to unlock them is the subject of a later chapter.

At this stage in your development your mother's attitude towards you is going to be of paramount importance. Whilst you are inside your mother's womb you are capable of picking up her moods and feelings via neurohormonal changes and the most important feeling of all is how she feels about you. There are four possibilities at this stage. Either she is keen to have you and knows it, thinks she's ambivalent but is subconsciously keen, thinks she's ambivalent but is subconsciously not keen, or else she definitely knows she doesn't want you. Being the perceptive little critter you are, you can distinguish which one of the four it is and this will have great bearing on future events.

Mothers who are keen to have their babies have, statistically, the easiest pregnancies and the most trouble-free births. Their offspring tend to be both physically and emotionally healthier. The ambivalent but subconsciously keen mother tends to get a confused, apathetic and rather lethargic baby, and, according to Dr Gerhard Rothman of the University of Salzburg, the ambivalent but subconsciously unkeen mother stands a good chance of having a baby with gastro-intestinal problems.[4]

The last group, those mothers who know that they don't want the child, will tend towards difficult pregnancies and births. There is a high rate of premature births in this group because, subconsciously, the mother may try to expel the foetus, and babies will tend to be of low birth weight because their mothers are less likely to take good nutritional care. It is from this group that the highest proportion of emotionally disturbed babies come. After all, how would you feel if you spent nine months in an enclosed space where you were not wanted?

The next most important factor is how your mother feels about your father at that time. If the relationship is a happy and contented one, then the chances are that the pregnancy will proceed smoothly and you will be calm and happy in the womb. On the other hand, if the relationship is a stressful one, and particularly if there is any violence or abuse, either physical or verbal, involved, the baby is five times more likely to be jumpy and fearful. This is a major cause of physical and emotional damage to a baby inside the womb.

Short-term stress doesn't have much effect on a baby. On the other hand, long-term stress does.[5] Not only can such long-term stress cause physical and emotional damage to the child in the womb, but this damage will frequently be carried through into adult life, or until the individual becomes sufficiently enlightened to recognise and do something about it.

Interestingly, studies have also shown that babies in

the womb can detect whether or not there is any danger to the father at this time. The mother's neurohormonal system reflects her anxiety, and the baby has a greater chance of being born with physical problems, is likely to be emotionally volatile and suffer from increased anxiety or depression as he grows up. There is a whole generation of men and women in the world born between 1939 and 1945 who are prime candidates for these symptoms, their fathers having been involved in World War II while their mothers stayed at home worrying about their husbands' safety.

Do you know how your parents related to each other before your birth? It would be helpful if you did. Perhaps you could talk to them about it, explaining to them why you want to know. You may be able to gain a valuable insight into your present emotional and physical state if you know the answers to some of these questions. If you then feel that some of your present problems are a result of that early programming, then you should acknowledge this and affirm that you don't need to follow these particular behaviour patterns anymore.

Let us now try a visualisation, using any of the information that you may have learned from your parents. This is quite a long one, so you will need to put it on tape. Close your eyes and go through a relaxing exercise with your body. Now think back to a time before your birth. Imagine that you are your father or your mother. Your mother has just discovered that she is pregnant. Now think about these questions.

How are they feeling about the pregnancy?
Are they an emotionally stable couple?
Are they married? If so, for how long have they been married?
Is this baby (you) planned?

How long have they been waiting for you?
What changes will your birth make to their lives?
Will your mother have to give up her job?
Will she have to cope with a previous child while
    carrying you?
Is the house they live in big enough for you all?
What do their respective families feel about this preg-
    nancy?
What is the relationship between your mother and her
    mother like? (This one is especially important.)
How is your mother feeling about her looks at this
    time?
Does your mother feel good about herself?
Is she afraid?
Do you have any brothers or sisters?
How are they feeling?
Do they want you or are they jealous?

Now imagine you are inside your mother's womb.

How are you feeling?
What is it like in there?

Just take your time and feel yourself floating in the womb
and being the focus of all the varied emotions and sensations which surround you. When you are ready, come
back to present time and open your eyes.

How did that feel? Did you experience anything? The
conditions may not have been perfect for such an experiment, but if you would like to try it more seriously find a
counsellor who deals in past lives to help you. There are a
lot of them around these days and any copy of one of the
New Age magazines will carry advertisements for them.

In cases of long-term stress baby may become hooked on
the adrenalin that is created by Mum's constant anxiety. If

great surges of adrenalin are a part of baby's everyday life in the womb, then it is likely that in later life he is going to feel comfortable with high adrenalin levels and will probably grow up seeking the sorts of thrills and excitements that will produce such levels. The daredevil baby is often the product of a highly anxious mother.

It has also been shown that babies in the womb can actually be taught to do certain things. One test which was reported in the *Journal of Experimental Psychology* involved teaching 16 babies to respond to gentle vibration by kicking.[6] Normally a baby wouldn't bother to react to gentle vibrations such as these but the researchers accompanied the vibrations in the early stages with a loud noise, something which was guaranteed to make the baby jump and kick. After a while they stopped using the noise but by then the babies had become conditioned to kick whenever they sensed the vibration.

Another learned response that has been shown in babies in the womb is related to the mother's intake of such potentially harmful products as drugs, caffeine, nicotine or alcohol. Of course at this stage the baby has no way of knowing what a cup of coffee or a cigarette is, but he does know that whenever Mum lights up, his oxygen supply is going to suffer. Very quickly he can make a connection between his mother's action and his own discomfort. If Mum is a regular smoker, then it isn't going to be long before baby is in a state of permanent apprehension wondering when his air supply is next going to be cut. The result might well be that the child will be born with a naturally anxious disposition and will go through life wondering when the next life-threatening thing is going to happen to him.

As well as the physical, the emotional side of personality also starts to form in the womb. If Mum allows her own emotions free rein, then her baby is going to start learning certain lessons. Small doses of anger, sadness, fear or extreme rage will produce different sensations in the child, but as long as mother is reasonably well balanced emotionally, and still has a basic love for the child she is carrying, then the baby will quickly begin to realise that such emotions are 'normal'. In fact there is a school of thought that says that a moderate amount of anxiety of one sort or another is good for an unborn child as it starts to condition him for life outside the womb by allowing him to begin building primitive defences against unpleasant external forces. [7]

A complete absence of emotion in the foetus's life, be it good or bad emotion, is basically negative. It is not the presence of upsetting emotions which matter but what we, as adults, do about them. For example, brief outbursts of anger followed by relaxation and love tell a baby that anger is safe. Anger that is bottled up and followed by long periods of hate and resentment will set a similar pattern in the baby and may result in later childhood problems.

Through the work of Dr Peter Fedor-Fraybergh, Professor of Obstetrics and Gynaecology at the University of Uppsala in Sweden, we learn that expectations are also formed in the womb at this time. If, for example, the womb is a warm, safe and pleasant place to be, then the baby is likely to expect the outside world to be likewise. On the other hand, if the experience in the womb is one of constant challenge, then baby is likely to expect that the outside world will present the same challenges and may not be so keen to join it.

The important thing throughout is that the mother still feels basically good about the child. If at any stage throughout the pregnancy this love is withdrawn from the child, then, as we have seen previously, the child is liable to be withdrawn himself and is likely to suffer from some emotional instability.

Of course, the other important aspect of personality and character is your sexuality. This is something else with which we all usually come into contact whilst still in the womb. Most doctors agree these days that sexual activity can continue in pregnancy until it becomes uncomfortable for the mother. The result is that the baby can become used at an early stage to the emotional and physiological changes that overtake Mum's body during orgasm. After a while these, like the other daily emotions, will be accepted as 'normal'. It is possible, according to the research of Dr Thomas Verny, an American psychiatrist, that if your mother felt sexual about her pregnancy, the actual process of childbirth and subsequent breastfeeding, then your own sexuality will be strong and positive. Sexuality can be adversely affected if your time in the womb was one of almost constant terror.

It's not hard to tell what a foetus dislikes, he shows it strongly enough by behaving like the front-row forward of a rugby team. Yelling, Heavy Metal rock music and parents fighting are high on the list of dislikes. Usually the degree of kicking will tell you the state of baby's mind at the time. He can also be most annoyed if he is forced into an uncomfortable position and will kick to tell you to turn over. This will be translated after birth into his 'I'm angry' cry, as will his reaction to raised voices and other dislikes which were formed in the womb.

To sum up then, it is clear that there is a strong communication link between mother and baby which goes beyond the physical. Happy, contented mothers-to-be are far more likely to produce lively, easy-going offspring than emotionally-distressed, anxious mothers are.

# LEARNING TO SURVIVE

Contrary to beliefs which were held by psychologists and other assorted childcare experts for hundreds of years it now seems that the first three years of life are the most important years, formatively speaking, for a child. By the age of seven the major subconscious programming has been done, a fact which, incidentally, was not unknown to the Jesuits who, as long as 500 or more years ago, were saying 'Give us a child until he is seven and after that you can do what you like with him'. They realised very early on the significance of those early formative years.

There are an extraordinary number of influences which, along with the in-the-womb conditioning discussed in the previous chapter, help to create the groundwork for adult behaviour.

The actual experience of birth, your relationships with your mother and father, whether or not you were breastfed, how much you were touched and handled, the reactions you received to your baby behaviour, your family environment and the kind of conditioning you received, all helped you to form your positive and negative beliefs about yourself and the world, and to make decisions about how you would deal with certain areas of your later life, including your health and sexuality.

Much of this, as we know, is stored in the subconscious and directs our future behaviour without our realising it. Mostly belief patterns in your subconscious move silently, like a stage manager in the wings, but sometimes they can be resurrected by powerful sense stimulus. What is the earliest memory you have of your childhood? Can you remember as far back as one year old? Two, maybe? Or three? We know one man who, at the age of forty, was walking down the street one day and came across a council gang laying a new road. The strong smell of the tar-making machine caused him suddenly to remember an occasion in his childhood when he was just three years old, an occasion which he had not recalled in thirty-seven years! Smell is a particularly good sense for jolting the memory. Sound is another. For some reason, sight, the most obvious sense for most of us, is probably the worst of all when it comes to helping us recall the past.

The birth experience, as well as being extremely painful for the baby, is also a very sensual one. After nine months of floating around in a pool of amniotic fluid, birth is the first real experience the child has of physical contact and sensuality which, to some degree, will affect his adult sexuality. The more pleasant the birth, the more likely the child is to have a well-balanced emotional attitude in later life. The more unpleasant the birth, the geater the likelihood that the child will grow up with either an unhealthy attitude towards physical contact and sex or a general disinterest in it. Other negative attitudes may also be caused by a difficult birth: for example the attitude that life is a dangerous thing, or the baby perhaps may develop a fear of men if a man delivered the child. Find out from your mother which type of birth you had.

Induced births present particular problems for mother and baby. It is generally at the insistence of the doctor that a birth is induced. Of course there are all sorts of genuine concerns that doctors have about their patients (they will insist on calling pregnant mothers 'patients' as though they are sick!) which require induction, but it is rare that such action is really vital. Induction is brought about by intravenously pumping an artificial oxytocin into the mother's blood stream which will start her uterus contracting. Neither mother nor baby is really ready for birth at this time and it is generally an unsatisfactory exercise for them both. In fact many mothers say that they don't feel as though they are part of the process but that it is being forced on them. They find it hard to follow the contractions and feel that they are no longer in control of the birth. Studies have shown that this experience may have an adverse effect on the child's personality in later life, too.

During rebirthing sessions we have come across many people whose anger or depression in adult life have been attributable to a painful birth. Unable to externalise that anger, they have turned in on themselves and that one simple, but unpleasant, action of being born has become a major factor in the formation of their entire personality throughout their lives. Unaware of the reasons, they have gone through life unhappy or depressed. Doctors will probably have prescribed pills which will have done little or no good and all because the cause of this unhappiness lies in the process of birth.

What then if you happen to have been a Caesarian birth? You would have been spared any possible pain going down the birth canal, but denied any pleasure as well. Does this mean that you are therefore free from trauma? Unfortunately not!

Medical intervention in birth is increasing at an alarming rate in the Western world. Doctors claim that with modern technology they are able to detect sooner than before if a baby is in trouble and by quickly performing an operation on the mother they can save the child's life. In days gone by the baby would probably have died. This sounds fine, but so far nobody has been able to produce any real figures to show that these claims are actually true. In the meantime doctors are increasingly performing Caesarian sections, with all the risks that surgery involves — the physical risks and the emotional risks that attend a baby born by Caesarian section.[1] Having missed out on the first, and possibly most important, sensual experience of their lives, these babies, according to Dr Thomas Verney, may end up having disorganised feelings about sex and physical contact with others. Sometimes, too, these babies aren't fully aware of their physical proportions with the result that they can be very clumsy. It's rather like being taught to drive in a VW Beetle and then quite suddenly being asked to negotiate the rush-hour in a huge Cadillac!

The most common result of a Caesarian birth is that the child grows up demanding a lot of physical contact. They want to be held and cuddled a lot and will tend to touch you when they talk to you. This is the subconscious desire for that tactile experience which they were denied at birth and which all of us need to feel secure. You can try your own mini experiment on this if you like. The next time you are at a party and you meet someone who is for-ever holding your arm or trying to touch you as you speak, ask them if they were a Caesarian birth. If nothing else it will open up a whole new avenue of conversation and it sure beats the hell out of talking about the weather!

Interference in the mother-baby birthing process may well flow through into early childhood. Bonding between the two may be harder and the experience may well have an adverse effect on the child's personality. Bonding is an important event and is the cementing of the relationship, both physical and emotional, between mother and baby, in the outside world. Study after study has shown that women who bond well became better mothers and their babies are almost always physically healthier and emotionally more stable. It is a two-way street if both parties are given a proper chance. Immediately after birth three important things happen if the baby is placed on Mum's breast. Firstly the baby's cries help to stimulate the flow of milk in the breasts, secondly the friction of baby's skin against the mother's breast stimulates a hormone which will stop Mum bleeding, and thirdly the closeness of the baby stimulates a maternal feeling in the mother. Ideally these important stimulations should take place immediately after birth as they cannot easily be recreated if the baby is taken away and only returned to the mother some time later.

On the other side of the coin, during the bonding process the baby feels that he is protected, loved, wanted and generally cared for. If the bonding is successful it generally means that the relationship between mother and child will be much easier, and, among other things, it is likely to minimise the possibilities of subsequent child abuse by the mother.

Ideally bonding should take place within the first twelve hours after birth, but do not despair if you are about to have a baby, or have just had one, and events have precluded this. It is not the end of the world. It is possible to bond with your child after this time, otherwise no mother would ever bond with a premature child who has to be kept in a humidicrib and that, as we know, is nonsense. However there is little doubt that the earlier you can do it the better for all concerned.

In extreme cases where there is absolutely no bonding between mother and baby a condition called marasmus may develop. The baby who receives no love and affection, no hugs, cuddles or kisses and is totally ignored is liable to pine away and die. This is thought to be one of the major causes of foundling deaths and can occur even once the baby has been 'rescued', fed and clothed. But again don't despair. There are thousands of mothers who find it hard to bond with their baby for ages, if indeed ever, yet they still manage to have a perfectly passable life together.

So that fathers don't feel left out at this stage, we should mention the male equivalent of bonding which is called engrossment. Fathers should spend as much time as early as possible with their newborn baby so that the same sort of bond can be formed between them. There is no doubt that fathers who have been present at the birth and have spent a lot of time with the newborn form a much stronger relationship with their child than fathers who were absent at birth and spend little time with the newborn. Incidentally those fathers who participate more also tend to make life easier for the mother, with the result that harmony in the home is greater and the child grows up in a better atmosphere. Did your father take time to bond with you? Find out, if you can, how much time he spent with you after you were born and measure that against the closeness of your relationship today. The two are generally connected.

Together Mum and Dad will supply the stimuli which are needed for a newborn baby to grow into a healthy toddler. Mum will probably supply the loving, caring, feeding, bathing and general looking after that a baby needs, plus much of the basic discipline. Dad will probably supply the fun, excitement, gymnastics and general stimulation which is also needed to keep a baby alert and mentally and physically exercised.

Human beings, for all their extraordinary physiological makeup, are about the most physically backward of all species when it comes to the newborn. A human baby can do just about nothing for itself and will continue in this state of helplessness for quite a long time. It is supposedly nature's way of saying that humans are civilised enough to look after their young and there is no such immediate threat of danger to life and limb as there is for baby animals in the wild.

Cast your mind back if you can to those days when you were a baby and absolutely helpless. You can move but all your muscles are like Aeroplane jelly, your fingers won't work for you, you cannot speak or write and therefore have difficulty in making others understand your needs. In fact about all you can do is laugh (a little) and cry (a lot). You quickly develop different cries to suit different situations. You have your 'I'm hungry' cry and your 'I'm cold' cry and, of course, your 'I'm frightened' cry. That's just about all the communication you have and you are totally and utterly dependent on others for your survival.

Try to recreate that feeling in your mind now. Imagine what it would be like. You are a stranger in a strange world about which you know nothing. You have absolutely no idea what is going to happen to you from one minute to the next and you cannot be sure that there is going to be anyone there to help you. You have no idea whether anyone is going to come if you cry, or what it is that might make people abandon you altogether.

You are surrounded by giants who do all sorts of things to you against which you have no defence. They pick you up and pass you around. They stuff food of one sort or another into your mouth whether you feel hungry or not. They dunk you in water whether you feel like it or not. They put clothes on you without any real idea of whether you are feeling too hot or too cold. They make noises over you relative to a variety of emotions which they may feel and understand but about which you know nothing. In short, you are in the Land of Giants and absolutely at their mercy. How does that make you feel? Are you feeling safe? Are you afraid? What sort of strategies can you work out to protect yourself?

One thing becomes quickly obvious to you as a new-born child. Since you are entirely dependent on these big people it makes sense to try to please them, otherwise they may go off and leave you on your own to fend for yourself. So what do you do? Well, it's a question of trial and error. You do something, a laugh maybe or a smile, and it gets a positive result. Suddenly people are crowding round you giving you lots of love and attention and giving off masses of positive vibes. 'Ah ha', you think, 'that's obviously a good trick. I'll try that one again'. On the other hand you may try something else and the result is the opposite, you feel people getting cross with you and going away. The chances are you won't repeat that behaviour again in a hurry.

As you get older you repeat this pattern. Whilst as a baby you are totally helpless, as a toddler you have a little more control over your life but you are still basically dependent on the giants. Most of the things that you need to make life really comfortable for yourself have to be provided by the big people so, by and large, you go on ensuring that you please them enough to get the things you want. In short you learn by your results. You don't necessarily understand very much about what you or other people are doing, but you have learnt the lesson of cause and effect and this will stay with you forever.

As you pass into adulthood you are still likely to stick with the old system of 'What will give me the results I want?' The only trouble is that in adult life it doesn't always work quite so well. For example, you ask someone to do something for you and they forget. You get cross with them and it results in an argument. You may prove that you were right but does that lead them to doing it for you the next time? The answer is probably not! Babies are often instinctively smarter than adults!

So what has all this to do with your health? Well, let's see. Get a piece of paper and write down now a chronological history of all your health problems starting as far back as you can remember. Don't forget all the measles and mumps, the fevers and flu and other passing ailments. When you have done that ask yourself the following question: 'In what ways did I benefit from being ill as a child. . .?' It could be something like developing a bad attack of asthma for example in order to get out of having to play football, or you might have contracted something like glandular fever so that your mother would spend more time fussing over you. Make a note of all the insights you may have just had about how you could have benefited from being sick.

Your view of the world, including health, will depend on the reactions which you got in your early life. For example, if you got attention whenever you wanted it, when you cried or when you were happy, you are likely to have come to the conclusion that the world is a pretty safe place to be in and that love will come to you independent of your needs. If occasionally your needs were met with a degree of irritation, or after a delay but followed by hugs, then you probably would conclude that you might not always get what you want when you want it, but that you are still loved. You will learn that it is okay to have needs, and to ask for those needs to be fulfilled, but that you will not always have them met. The results overall would be that you would grow up as a basically healthy child.

If, on the other hand, nobody paid any attention to you at all when you were quiet and only made a fuss of you when you cried you would probably come to the speedy conclusion that in order to get some love and attention it was necessary to cry a lot. This could lead on to the sub-conscious realisation that becoming ill or needy brought you love or attention. However, if, when you cried and made a fuss, your parents got angry and frustrated with you, you may have bottled up your feelings in order not to risk losing your parents' approval. After all you were still dependent on them for your survival so you could not risk doing anything that might cut off your lifeline. You learnt just how powerless you were and that you had no control over your life. The result of these circumstances is that you either deliberately choose illness in order to attract some love and attention or you bottle it all up inside you and become ill that way instead. Either way will lead to physical and emotional problems.

It is important that a baby gets some impression of being able to control at least a small part of his life. This gives him confidence and a confident baby is generally a healthy baby. To give an example, if you are playing with a six-week-old baby and he sticks his finger in your nose you should let out a quick sharp snort. The baby will pull back then, intrigued, like a puppy with a snail, he will venture the finger again. He is rewarded with another quick snort. Soon the baby will learn that every time he puts his finger up your nose he elicits this funny noise. He is actually in control, he believes. He is causing this reaction.

Since a baby's only yardstick is the reaction that he gets from other people it is important to react visibly to whatever he tries to do. This becomes even more important as the child grows older. If a toddler attempts to do something and gets no reaction from you for his effort he will soon believe that he cannot achieve whatever it is and give up. This is known as 'enforced helplessness' and is often the reason why children cannot read, or tell the time, or write properly when all their peers are achieving these milestones. By ignoring the child you are enforcing his belief that he is helpless when it comes to specific tasks and he will give up on them.

If this is allowed to develop too far the child could grow up believing that he is generally helpless and so will depend on others for his survival throughout his life. He will display a helpless attitude to attract the assistance he needs. Frequently this will take the form of a variety of illnesses, often quite serious ones, to reinforce the image of being in need of help.

Another very important hurdle you had to face in early childhood was food. Since all delivery systems of food in those early days were beyond your control, but were vital for your continued survival, a number of factors became important. Firstly came the question of whether you were being fed or not. Clearly if you were not being fed and were hungry, then you were going to view the world as a desperately unsafe place. And the people who were meant to be supplying you with food would seem wholly unreliable and potentially dangerous to your welfare and therefore to be viewed with suspicion. Then there is the question of the sort of emotions which surrounded feeding times. Was it an easy-going, relaxed, friendly atmosphere or was feeding always done in a great stressful rush? Did Mum enjoy the feeding ritual or was it a matter of extreme irritation — something that should be got over with the greatest of speed and minimum of fuss?

Surveys have shown that babies who were breastfed by their mothers in a quiet, relaxed and loving way were more likely to have a well-balanced attitude towards food. Those whose mothers went through the process without any enjoyment, or who felt embarrassed, rushed or un-comfortable about it, often associated food (and the person feeding them) with negative thoughts which could follow through into later life.

Another common problem lies with the breastfeeding mother who smokes or drinks to excess and therefore taints the milk. This often results in the baby feeling he cannot trust the quality of the food which again leads to mistrust of the provider. Once again the child will have negative attitudes about food in general which can lead to ill-health in later life. This may manifest itself, in severe cases, in the adult starving themselves, for example, (anorexia nervosa), or in compulsive eating and elimination (bulimia); or perhaps the adult may subconsciously only trust certain foods, which can lead to nutritional imbalances and, hence, diseases of deficiency.

When it comes to the question of when the baby should be weaned off the breast and on to the bottle there are conflicting opinions. However try looking at it this way. Imagine you are a baby again and have been having lots of lovely warm, cosy meals with your Mum. Suddenly one day without warning you are denied the warmth of your mother's breast and a nasty rubber teat smelling of disinfectant is put in your mouth. How would you feel? The abrupt cessation of breastfeeding, which can be brought about by a number of circumstances like the mother going back to work or being ill or simply just wanting a break from the routine, can be equated in some instances with a loss of love and security. The baby may suddenly feel unwanted, which may result in him becoming a more clinging child. If, on the other hand, you allow the child to wean himself off the breast he is more likely to feel secure, confident and independent because he is in control.

And what if you were bottle-fed from the start? Well, that's a whole different ball game. The answer is that as long as mother and baby have a good bonded relationship, then it really doesn't matter a whole heap emotionally if the baby is breast or bottle-fed. There is no doubt that breast feeding a child helps to bond the two more quickly, but it is equally possible to do it without, so there is no need to feel unduly guilty if you opted for the bottle with your babies. If you happen to have been a bottle-fed baby yourself think back on your relationship with your mother and see if you can notice any negative attitudes towards food which may have resulted. It's unlikely. Mind you, the nutritional story is another matter.

# CHAPTER 6
# STICKS AND STONES...AND FAMILY LIFE

By the time you reach the age of seven you will have learnt quite a lot about life. You have learnt, for example, that the big people who look after you probably aren't going to abandon you just because you do certain things which they don't like. This encourages you to experiment and do more of these things, like throwing the vegetables all over the kitchen floor or trying to flush the cat down the loo! But the closer it gets to meal time the better your behaviour becomes because you know that you still need them for the basics of comfortable living.

By now, too, children will have come to some basic and long-lasting decisions about health and illness. For example they will probably have learnt that when they are sick they are put to bed with a warm drink and Mum makes a big fuss over them. This could lead to the discovery that a successful way to get their mother's attention at any time is to be ill and they may well make themselves ill in the years to come for just that reason.

They may also have made up their mind about relationships. Based largely on the sort of relationship that their parents have, they will decide whether or not it is safe to get close to Mum and Dad and men and women in general. They will have made some fairly basic decisions about their brothers and sisters. Their sexuality will also be developing by this age, and they will either be feeling pretty confident about being a boy or girl or feeling fairly insecure.

In short, the sorts of experiences that you have as you grow up in your first seven years will affect your decisions about what sort of person you are going to be and what sort of behaviour you are going to avoid. Much, if not all of this is, of course, unconscious; still, some decisions are definitely made consciously. For example, you may have been greatly embarrassed by your mother when you were small because she always insisted on picking you up and kissing you profusely in front of your friends. You might have vowed at that time never to embarrass your children in that way, or perhaps never to show that sort of emotion in public, if at all. You might have decided that any expression of emotion was a bad thing which led to unpleasantness, so consequently you swore to yourself that you would never let others see how you were feeling. These and many other decisions made at that time you will carry into later life, and live them out, whether or not they are appropriate for you at that future stage. They will be so embedded in your subconscious that the chances are you will not even know they are there.

Think back now to your own childhood. Can you consciously remember any of the decisions that you may have made at that time? Was there anyone in your life then that you swore you wouldn't be like when you grew up? Or conversely, was there anyone whom you worshipped and set out to be like? Did you ever feel that it was up to you to make other people feel good with the result that your own feelings were played down? Many of today's best healers started out that way, you know. Their early childhood decision was that it was their role to help others and that their own emotional needs and desires were of no importance. They were loved and praised when they were helpful, and so ended up believing that they were loved for what they did rather than who they were.

All these decisions are bound to have a limiting effect on your behaviour today. They are bound to increase your stress level subconsciously and will almost certainly have a detrimental effect on your health unless you take time out to examine them and discard the ones which are clearly out of date and serving no useful purpose. For example, if you were one of those who made the childhood decision not to indulge in public displays of emotion, you are likely to feel stressed and under pressure whenever anyone does behave in that way, particularly if it is directed towards you. Obviously, if your partner or child expresses emotion to you in public you will find difficulty in responding (often without understanding the reason why) and this may have a damaging effect on your relationships.

And how did we arrive at these decisions that so influence our adult lives? They are formed by a combination of factors. There are those we have already discussed: our temperament, pre-birth conditioning and early childhood learning via observation and a primitive recognition of the relationship between cause and effect. But there is another influence during our childhood which profoundly affects the developing pattern of our lives — and this includes our health because, after all, our state of health forms the ever present backdrop to our existence. This major influence is childhood conditioning.

As a child you receive one of two types of message. The first type will basically coincide with your own desires and needs, and the second type will conflict with those. Clearly your initial desires and needs are predominantly to be yourself, to exist, to feel, to think, to grow, to be a child, to grow up, to be as close or as independent as you want at any given moment, to follow your own inclinations, to enjoy yourself in your own way, to have your own hobbies, your own sexual inclinations and follow your own career.

If you are, by and large, allowed to follow your chosen pattern, then you will most probably feel that it is quite safe to be yourself and you can explore the world from a position of safety. The chances are that you will have a long, happy, and above all healthy life, always assuming that you aren't cut off in your prime by a pygmy blow pipe!

The other kind of message however creates all sorts of problems for you. This message is predominantly telling you that you have to be different, that you cannot be yourself and cannot do and think the things that you want to do and think.

Sometimes these messages take the form of 'instructions' that are specifically designed to limit your behaviour so that it fits into the accepted social conduct.

Think back to your childhood again and write down a list of all the instructions you can remember getting from your parents. Perhaps you were told that you shouldn't pick your nose or that you shouldn't talk at the dinner table. Perhaps your mother told you that if you didn't eat your vegetables you'd get scurvy, or your father may have said that you would never be a success in life if you didn't learn all your mathematical tables.

Now add to that all the criticisms that were levelled at you by your parents and your uncles and aunts, cousins, brothers and sisters. Can you remember them? Your nose was too big or your toes were deformed or your voice was too squeaky. As you grew up teachers, neighbours and friends may have joined in this chorus of criticism. Of course no-one was trying to be nasty. These were all little criticisms designed to 'help' you make the best of yourself. After all, how could you improve if you weren't aware of your faults?!

Normal exploratory behaviour may have been prohibited. For example, you may have been prevented from touching yourself. If, as a child, you were actively stopped from touching your genitals (a perfectly normal and harmless pursuit) it could have repercussions on your sexuality today.[1] You may also have felt, at this early age, that your mother didn't want you to take any pleasure out of life. Remember that a small child's sphere of reference is very limited and a simple action like being stopped from playing with yourself can be translated into a whole generalised belief.

Generally speaking, if you are attacked, blamed or criticised as a child one of two things will happen. You either turn inwards or outwards. Turning inwards you will decide that you are powerless over the world and will feel worthless. You will learn to put up with things and become obedient, and you will be thought of as such a good child. You will, however, have relinquished all your own power to others and the more you are criticised the more powerless you will become. Even passive rebellion is still a form of powerlessness because in this case you have given up the power to express your feelings or to defend yourself. On the other hand, if you turn outwards you will fight back at your detractors and become aggressive. You will be termed a rebel, whereas, in fact, all you are doing is exercising your right to be yourself! In terms of your own emotional and physical health it is probably preferable to be the latter type. Bottled-up emotions are never a good thing.

Childhood patterning is such a powerful influence that the chances are you are probably still doing the same things today as an adult that you did as a child, even if you know them to be inappropriate for you! Now is the time to look at your list and see if you can relate any of the instructions and criticisms to some of your beliefs today. Are these beliefs of any use to you now or can you afford to discard them? After all, if they are outdated or irrelevant they are only going to hold you back. List the patterns in your life that you would like to change. To change them, create the necessary affirmations and start working through them one by one. There is absolutely no need any more to hold on to all those outdated, inappropriate ideas.

Then there were those messages that were not given to help you improve yourself. In fact, they were probably not meant to be instructional messages at all. Yet they still have deep psychological effects that limit our behaviour in every area of our lives.

One of the strongest messages of this sort that a child can receive is the 'Don't exist' message. It may start with an unwanted pregnancy and a mother saying something like: 'If it wasn't for you coming along I wouldn't have had to give up my career'. Then there's the other common one, the financial guilt trip: 'If it hadn't been for you I could have gone on working and we would have had more money so that we could live in a better house'. Or else there's the 'If it hadn't been for you I could have divorced your father' scenario. If one of these, or something similar, was practised on you, they all come to much the same thing — don't exist!

Then there's that ridiculous old Victorian adage, 'children should be seen and not heard'. The Victorians were pastmasters at filling their children with complexes. This particular one simply says 'If you must be here the least you can do is sit quietly in a corner and pretend that you aren't.'

The orders not to be a nuisance and to do as you are

told are also both negative messages that you might have received during childhood. Basically what you were being told is that you have no place thinking for yourself. Life will be a lot more peaceful for your parents if you simply let them do it all. This is a great way to stifle imagination and creativity in a child who, though he may be creating havoc in your dirty clothes basket and making extra work for you, is in fact experimenting with his new-found world.

'Keep out of the way' is another common order and that's sometimes coupled with 'Be careful not to upset anyone'. Both messages suggest that, unless you are very careful, your own safety may be in jeopardy. So rather than pop up and be your usual jovial, mischievous self you go and hide in your bedroom when visitors come round.

How many times have you heard parents say to their child 'Oh for God's sake, grow up!'? This happens with depressing frequency, unfortunately. What this is saying to the child is 'Stop being a child because your vulnerability is making me nervous'. This is particularly common with the first child in a family. The corollary of this is 'I never want you to grow up', usually aimed at the youngest child when a mother realises that she isn't going to have any more children and her opportunity for pleasure in maternity is fast running out. Either way, the child is basically being told to stop being himself.

There are also more subtle messages that parents can give their children. One of the most common is the 'Be the other sex' message. This is usually done by giving the child an ambivalent name. For example, you really wanted a boy but you got a girl so you called her Peta or you gave her a girl's name like Josephine but insisted on calling her Jo. Is there anything ambivalent about your name? Think about it!

There is a whole range of other equally destructive messages which often were given to you quite subconsciously by your parents and which are almost impossible to recall. If you have the right sort of relationship with your parents, try asking them (in a forgiving and understanding way!) some of these questions and find out what sort of a response you get.

The trouble with 'don't exist' messages is that you don't always realise that you are being given them, but you react to them nevertheless. If they are particularly strong you may react by subconsciously giving yourself a fatal illness. After all, what better way not to exist than to die? You may do something slightly less radical like putting yourself into dangerous situations on the off-chance that you might get wiped out. This is a common pattern in war correspondents. The job usually attracts men and women who have a particularly strong death urge. It is often very hard to get them away from the front once they have had their first taste of battle. In fact, if your life urge is less than your death urge, you are likely to be drawn to drinking and driving, or working in a leper colony, or becoming a mountaineer or a racing driver — anything which carries a high element of risk with it, even though you may only be conscious of other motivations such as a sense of duty or altruism, or a desire for new experiences. Let's look at a couple of actual case histories which illustrate how childhood messages can affect your whole life.

Case 1: There were two sisters, Jane and Mary, who came from a reasonably well-off family. Their father worked for a computer company and their mother had been an illustrator before she gave up work to look after her children. Jane, the eldest, was a healthy girl who excelled at sport of all kinds. She generally outshone her younger sister who was somewhat timid and felt that Jane bullied her. Jane was forever roping Mary into games of all sorts, and particularly to go swimming, which the younger girl hated.

She couldn't play any of the games very well, would often get hurt, and was terrified of water. One day when Jane was trying to get Mary to take part in a swimming afternoon, their mother said sternly 'Jane, stop bullying your sister to play with you, you know she's got a bad cold'. Jane left Mary alone and Mary suddenly realised that she could escape this problem if she was ill. Heartened by this revelation Mary started to make a subconscious habit of becoming ill whenever a situation was likely to arise which she wanted to avoid. The result was that she grew up feeling safe when she was sick and rather vulnerable when she was well. Inadvertently her mother had given her the message that illness was a way of escaping some of the unpleasant facts of life.

Case 2: Simon attended the local high school. He was an average student who didn't like school much. He generally came around the middle of his class, never shone in anything that he did and had relatively few friends. At the end of one term he heard his parents discussing his school report, which was worse than usual. His mother was bemoaning the fact that her only son seemed to be falling behind the rest of the class and was achieving so little. In his defence, Simon's father pointed out that he had been very ill that winter and hadn't been able to study properly, so it was little wonder that his school report was so poor. Overhearing this Simon suddenly realised that illness was a 'safe' reason for not achieving and he subconsciously countered every challenge to his progress by becoming sick. When the time came for him to leave school, it was suggested that he should follow in his father's footsteps and study to become a mechanical engineer. Simon realised that this was beyond him, so he started to make himself ill in order to get out of going to technical college. Later on he got married and when his wife started to put pressure on him to move to another part of the country he once again countered the challenge by becoming ill, making it necessary for them to stay where they were. In fact every time there was any sort of pressure in Simon's life his answer was to make himself ill so that he did not have to face up to it. He had a 'reasonable' excuse to avoid the issue, and all this because once, when he was fourteen years old, he had overheard his father telling his mother that being ill was an acceptable excuse for not achieving or not living up to someone else's expectations!

Such messages can be delivered in the most casual way but cause the deepest effect on the subconscious. They don't even necessarily have to be delivered to you; they can be delivered to a third person but taken to heart by you and your behaviour will adjust accordingly. A simple example of this occurred when Kathleen was young. One of her aunts happened to say to her mother one day 'Doesn't Kathleen knit nice and tightly'. Soon afterwards Kathleen noticed that, quite unconsciously, her knitting had become even tighter still! Translate that to a behavioural situation and you can see what can happen quite easily.

The decision is not necessarily a conscious one, nor is it necessarily 'wrong'. In fact, in a society in which it is acceptable to be physically sick but often unsafe to express emotional needs or be mentally sick, you have found a very sensible, very safe, and socially condoned way of getting your needs met. Well done! The only problem is that you are now sick!

So it is possible that as a child you can acquire a disease in order to avoid something that is expected of you but which you either do not wish to do or which you know you cannot live up to. It may be that you are artistically minded and have your heart set on becoming a painter when you grow up, but your family have always been army people and your father is expecting you to follow the tradition and join the armed forces. Perhaps you have it in mind to become an interior decorator but everyone is pressuring you to join the family grocery business! In such circumstances you might well develop an illness which would preclude you from following the path being forced on you.

The family environment has a lot to do with this sort of outcome and different families encourage different personalities in their children. For example, there are those families where the stiff upper lip is the order of the day. If you fall over and graze your knee you know there's no point running to Mummy crying because she'll tell you to stop being such a baby. Alternatively there are the families where it is perfectly acceptable to display emotion whenever appropriate and crying is considered okay by both the male and female members of the household.

Believe it or not illness is often judged in much the same way as emotion. There are certain illnesses which are acceptable to a particular family and others which are not. For example, we know of one British family where the teenage son was forever retiring to bed with recurring asthma and received a great deal of fuss and attention from everyone when he did. However, when the daughter, who was several years older, contracted an unusual tropical disease she had picked up in South America and which left her bed-ridden for several months, she was shunned by many members of her family. In a different family things could well have been the other way about. The parents may well have told their son to stop being a layabout and get himself healthy but made a big fuss of the daughter when she suddenly went down with this unusual and frightening disease.

This idea of giving yourself an illness in order to avoid something which you don't fancy, is a two-way street. You may have the desire to be as healthy as possible but still have illness foisted on you by your parents. Parents make their children ill for a number of reasons, but primarily because either they want to increase the child's dependence on them or they feel they need extra reasons to take care of them. It is possible, for example, for a mother who realises that she is one day going to lose her beloved only son to the big wide world and, horrors, to another woman, subconsciously to create an environment and set of situations whereby the boy will become ill and need his mother to look after him. If she does the job well enough he could very well be dependent on her for the rest of his life!

Alternatively the need for illness can exist equally in both parties. The mother needs a patient to care for and the child needs love and attention, or the father needs to feel that he is the powerful provider and the child needs to feel wanted and cared for.

A family's other emotional and physical habits can also be passed on. If, for example, both parents gain comfort and emotional protection from eating large amounts of food, then the chances are more than likely that they will have obese children. They will create exactly the same pattern in their children who, as frequently happens, may find a partner similar in make-up to themselves and pass it down to their children, and so on and so on. This family conditioning is extremely powerful. After all, the chances are that as a child you loved your parents. You trusted them and had an innate belief that whatever your parents did was right. You also know now that you survived your childhood, therefore your belief that whatever happened to you cannot have been too bad is strengthened. As a consequence you are likely to recreate the conditions of your childhood with your own children, feeling safe in the knowledge that, since you survived it, your children will survive it also.

For example, if your father used to take the strap to you when you were naughty you may arrive at the assumption that this sort of controlled violence is acceptable and so practise it on your own children as a means of discipline. If you were beaten up by your father regularly as a child, there is a good chance that you will come to feel that you can cope in violent surroundings after so many years of practice. The chances are that you will eventually create similar conditions around yourself. You might develop the sort of personality that is always looking to pick a fight with someone, or you may even take to !oitering in rough neighbourhoods in the knowledge that there's a good chance you'll get yourself involved in a punch-up. On the other hand, you may go to the other extreme and become passive and peace oriented.

The conditioning which your parents subject you to will pass on to your adult life and you will probably pass it down to your own children. If you were always being criticised for being selfish or thoughtless, you probably think that such behaviour is the only way to get attention and recognition. Therefore you may have become so in order to continue getting that response, this time from your spouse or your friends (if you have any!). People like this very often feel most uncomfortable when they are praised. Praise is not a commodity they have been used to and they can find it acutely embarrassing.

Let's finish this chapter with an exercise. Take a pen and write down as many completions to the following statements as you can:

A way I have created my life to mimic my childhood is...

A way my health as a child affected my activities is...

A way in which my parents encouraged me to be ill is...

# CHAPTER 7
# RATIONAL MAN VS COSMIC KOALA

At this point some of you may be wondering whether the whole business of choosing your own health, be it physical or emotional health, is really possible and not just some metaphysical claptrap. After all most of us have spent so much of our lives placing our faith in others that it has become as ingrained as the grooves on a long-playing record.

From the beginning, as we have seen, we have all been subjected to a barrage of external influences, all of which have in some way affected the development of our individual behaviour patterns. But, are we then left to stand by ourselves, rather like separate shags on separate rocks, from which we can choose and redefine our own destinies? No, because we have been conditioned in yet another way: frequently we have been taught to hand over responsibility for ourselves to an outside agent.

Throughout our lives we have been asked to put our faith in our parents, in our schoolteachers, the clergy, doctors and, above all, as we have seen in an earlier chapter, in God. Not often along the line has anyone bothered to stop us and say 'You must have faith in yourself before you can have faith in others'.

The result of this is that it can be daunting to be suddenly faced with a whole set of new hypotheses, such as those in this book, which require you to have absolute faith in yourself in order to solve them. You couldn't be blamed for wondering at this stage whether or not the whole thing is a load of hogwash and to go back to the old ways you have been taught and have practised from your birth.

Before you arrive at that conclusion, give yourself a fair chance. Literally thousands and thousands of people around the world have discovered that by taking control of their own lives they have been able to heal themselves of just about everything ranging from supposedly incurable cancer to unhappy marriages. To achieve this most of them have believed in just two sources of power — universal intelligence and themselves.

The concept of a universal intelligence is reasonably simple. It does not require you to believe in any form of orthodox religious teaching. It doesn't require you to believe in Jesus Christ or Buddha or Mohammed, or Ron Hubbard for that matter! All it does is require you to believe that there is a power greater than yourself, a creative power which, in its infinite omnipotence and omniscience, surrounds us all in an ever-present loving blanket. This power has the ability to provide for us and sustain us, yet does not interfere with free will or choice.

The first thing you have to do is drop all expectations, such as those caused by childhood conditioning. Don't make assumptions about life, but rather give yourself over to it and accept that whatever happens to you happens for a reason. If your belief in life and in yourself is strong enough you can achieve anything. In just the same way as the belief in Christ of the early Christian martyrs was so strong that they were prepared to be thrown to the lions and die for it, your belief in yourself and your life must be so strong that you are prepared to live for it. So often we have been taught to think of ourselves in a negative way that we feel that we don't deserve anything in life. If this is what you think, then you will have to look at the underlying causes for this belief. Look for where that pattern was formed in your early life so that you can understand what makes you believe it so strongly now. A good affirmation to counter this belief is: I am worthy to receive everything good anyone cares to give me. So start by dropping all your expectations and give yourself a chance at looking at your life from a new perspective.

The second thing to remember is relax — don't try too hard! Once your belief in yourself is strong enough everything will fall into place in its own good time. You cannot rush things and trying too hard will only breed discouragement when matters don't immediately come about the way you would like them to. Once again the key to the exercise is faith in yourself. Just be patient.

The third, and perhaps the most important, thing is use your inner senses. So many people are brought up with the old adage 'seeing is believing' ingrained in their minds that they find it hard to come to terms with anything they cannot immediately experience with one of their outer senses. Their belief is that if you cannot see it, touch it, smell it, taste it, or hear it, then it doesn't exist. But there is more to life than meets the eye. Try developing your inner senses. Try 'feeling' it through deep inner reflection. If you can 'feel' something, then it too can join your list of valid experiences in life. The trouble is that so many of us find it hard to get in touch with our instincts that this most important of all the senses is often denied to us when we need it most.

If you were looking at a large lump of cheddar cheese sitting all yellow and crumbly on a plate you wouldn't dream of denying it was there simply because you couldn't smell it, would you? Of course not, because another of your common backup senses, in this case sight, would support you in the belief that the cheese indeed existed. So why do we so often deny our sense of 'feeling'? Probably because it rarely has a backup. Allow yourself to feel a situation and be guided by that feeling in just the same way as you would allow yourself to be guided by your sense of smell, sight, hearing or touch. Once you develop as complete a faith in this sense as you have in the others, you will find it can be the most powerful of all. It is, in effect, your sixth sense — an expression often used by people who don't really realise what they are saying. When you say 'I just have a sixth sense about so and so', what you are really saying is 'I feel it to be so' and that sense of feeling is invariably your best and truest guide. It is that element in our make-up which we sometimes refer to as 'instinct'.

Since huge numbers of human beings on this planet are brought up in the belief that it is wrong for one reason or another to show their true emotions, they learn to repress them. Repressing emotions is like stuffing sausage meat into a skin — sooner or later the skin is going to burst from the excess of pressure. The more you stuff your emotions down into your inner self the greater the likelihood that there is going to be a very messy explosion at some later stage in your life. The results of long suppressed emotions can range from severe mental illness, through physical brutality towards others, to giving yourself a serious physical illness. If you doubt this, visit any one of the hundreds of mental hospitals we have to build and look at some of the case histories.

Another important step is to ask yourself questions.

Examine your experiences and work out how they might relate to other experiences in your life, and how they might have been influenced by past conditioning. There is no such thing as a random action. Everything that you do is done for a reason, whether you necessarily understand that reason or not. The trouble is that so many of us act without conscious thinking. Try and relate your actions to your thoughts and experiences. Ask yourself *why* did I do or say such and such? *what* made me do it? *where* did I get that reaction from? *when* was the first time I felt that way?

For example, you might be sitting with a group of friends enjoying a quiet drink and a chat when the person next to you suddenly says 'I really think that my husband is a complete and utter selfish pig'. You turn and reply sarcastically, 'It takes one to know one'. From then on it's on for young and old and the major row of the century has erupted with everyone in the group taking sides. Very shortly this pleasant little group has broken up in acrimony and gone its different ways.

For days, weeks or months after an incident like that you might harbour resentment against a number of members of that group, your friends, because of what they said and the way they reacted to your sarcastic reply. The argument may have become so bad that you might never see some of them again. You can accept that, because you have probably persuaded yourself that their reaction to you was uncalled for, and if they are going to be that stupid then you don't want them as friends anyway. But how many people stop to think about what they actually said and *why*?

Let's try to analyse this hypothetical case. The woman on your right started by making a statement, 'My husband is a complete and utter selfish pig'. She may have made this statement for a number of reasons. Her husband may have refused to help with the housework even though she was as exhausted as he from a hard week at work. He may have bought tickets for the theatre that night without consulting her and asking her what she would like to go and see. It could be for any number of reasons. One thing is certain however. Whatever the reason, the problem is hers. She believes that something her husband has done or said is selfish — and she says so. In her own eyes she has every right to make the statement.

The next thing that happened was you saying, 'It takes one to know one'. Now, why did you say that? Could it be because you don't like the woman very much and saw an opportunity to convey your dislike of her? If this is the case, *why* don't you like the woman? Who does she remind you of? When was the first time you felt that way about anyone? If you are absolutely honest with yourself your answer to these questions may be something like this: 'I dislike this woman because she is always complaining that other people ignore her. She reminds me of myself. The first time I remember complaining that nobody paid attention to me was as a small child when my mother refused to play with me. I resent my mother for doing that and making me feel unwanted. I dislike this woman because she reminds me of the rejection I got from my mother and my own subsequent feelings of being unwanted.'

Your reaction to the woman's comment is a sarcastic, throw-away line which starts a battle, which erupts into a war, and results in casualties on all sides. In fact what you were doing was reacting to something which you dislike in yourself and recognised in the other woman's statement. There is a useful expression, the origins of which have been lost in the wisdom of time: 'Never engage the mouth until the brain is in gear!' If you have the ability to ask yourself questions and seek the why, where, what and when of situations which face you, very often you can save yourself and others a great deal of unnecessary heartache. The more you do this the faster and better you become at it. The more honest you can be with yourself, the quicker you can process other people's actions and words. Had you been able to process that woman's comment fast enough, you would have realised that her problem was her husband — but that *your* problem was with her. You would wisely not have responded and the war would never have begun.

CHAPTER 8

# YOUR BODY IS YOUR HOME

Now that you have decided to have faith in yourself and have seen that if you ask yourself questions and *listen* to the answers, you can learn a great deal about the underlying motives for your behaviour, let's try the process on health. How are you feeling right at this moment? You can learn a lot from the present state of your body if only you are prepared to stop a while and listen to what it is telling you.

When we were born our bodies responded openly and intuitively to the environment around us and to our bodily needs. When we felt hungry we made it quite clear and either a breast or bottle was shoved in our mouth. When we needed to eliminate waste from our system, we did so without thought for the whys and wherefores. It seemed like such a natural thing to do that we just did it.

But then we began to grow up and one by one we learnt to block these instinctive actions. We started to do things by rote. Meal times were set and we couldn't expect to get a feed whenever we felt like it. It was made plain that no-one was going to tolerate us performing natural bodily functions wherever we fancied. There was a proper time and place for all that!

All sorts of normal bodily needs began to be catered for in an organised manner with the result that the body didn't always get quite what it wanted. The result was that it began to wear down. In short, it began to age. But the body isn't going to take all this lying down. No siree, it's going to put up something of a fight. When it is not totally at ease the body displays dis-ease, and disease is its way of telling us that we're not doing the right thing by it. So what do we do? Well, many people pump it full of drugs, which is a way of telling the body to shut up. For example, if you get a nasty headache your immediate reaction may well be to reach for the aspirin. Another reaction to pain or disease is to have an operation to remove the offending part instead of trying to understand the signals which it is sending you. But the body isn't stupid. It's organised a bit like a tribe of North American Indians. One Indian is sent up a hill to send a smoke signal that all is not well with the tribe and help is required. Along comes a scout from the US Cavalry and shoots the Indian. His place is immediately taken by a second Indian and, if necessary, by a third or fourth, and they will continue to send the signal until the proper help comes. Thus it is with our body. If the cavalry in the shape of a white-gowned surgeon kills off the first signaller, you can bet your boots that another signaller will be along in no time at all to keep sending the message. With any luck you might get the message through before too much of you has been dispensed with!

A very sad example of this involved an elderly woman who went to the doctor complaining of a pain in her stomach. Upon examination it was found that she was bleeding into her abdomen and the doctors decided that she should immediately have an operation. They whisked her into hospital and performed a hysterectomy, while at the same time removing both her ovaries and her appendix for good measure! For some months she was better, but then the pains returned. She went back to the doctors and again they diagnosed abdominal bleeding. Back into hospital she went and this time they decided she must have a bowel obstruction and they located a small twist in her lower intestine which they straightened. For some months afterwards she was all right but then the pain returned again. Back she went and for a third time abdominal bleeding was found. The surgeons removed almost three litres of blood from the abdominal cavity this time and found that her liver was covered with blood and fluid-filled cysts. They drained the cysts and hoped for the best. The pain was relieved for a while but soon returned. Yes, you've guessed it! This time they removed her spleen. In all the woman had six abdominal operations during which various parts of her body were irretrievably removed. It was four years before a doctor discovered that she was, in fact, suffering from scurvy and the only thing she needed was a megadose or two of Vitamin C![1]

This is unfortunately not an isolated case. Sometimes surgeons will remove the symptoms without being quite clear about the cause. The body, being composed of lots of faithful Indians, will sometimes provide new symptoms in the hopes that next time someone will look for the cause. So listen to your body. If it is trying to tell you something it is unwise to ignore it. Very often an illness is not the result of any physical aberration at all, but rather the result of an emotional one. It is the body's way of telling you that it has an emotional need which is not being met. Of course becoming well again means that you have to find other ways to meet these needs and this may, in some cases, encourage yet another illness.

Often the emotional need can be very deep seated and

hard to trace. It is not uncommon for patients who have thought themselves to be ill to go into a deep depression when told that there is actually nothing wrong with them. Likewise people who have been suffering from an illness can become depressed when the doctor triumphantly announces that they are cured! If you have those sorts of depression, then it is time to start searching for the unfulfilled needs in your life, those deep down emotional needs which aren't getting the attention they deserve.

Becoming ill can often be a cover for a completely different set of circumstances. For example, a man had a heart attack because he was frightened he was going to lose his job. By having a heart attack he had a valid reason for quitting his job before he was sacked although he would not have consciously planned it to be that way. Fear and consequent stress set off a series of reactions throughout the body that adversely affect the heart. This is now well understood thanks to the work of Hans Selye. The reactions include the effect of adrenalin and stress hormones on heart rate and blood pressure. Another example is the woman who developed cancer of the breast because it allowed her to stop being the one who always cared for everybody and have people care for her instead! Stress and worry (about others, including those you love) can adversely affect (weaken) the immune system, thus decreasing the immune system's vigilance, which may allow abnormal cells to survive and develop into diseases such as fully blown cancer.

Remember what we said earlier. None of this need be conscious and guilt or self-recriminations are inappropriate. All these people did was find a socially acceptable way of dealing with their needs in a society that is sympathetic to physical needs, but often intolerant of emotional weakness.

The sad thing is that none of this would be necessary if we were prepared to listen harder to what our bodies tell us. Instead of rushing off to the medicine cupboard or the operating theatre, stop and find out if there is another reason why you allowed yourself to develop the illness and then find out if there isn't perhaps a better way of dealing with the problem.

As we have said, drugs and operations successfully remove the symptoms of the illness, but because no attempt has been made to discover the actual cause, new symptoms are likely to crop up again at a later date.

If you are prepared to embrace this new belief system about your health (and we assume that you must at least be halfway interested in doing so or you wouldn't have read this far!), then consider the advantages. You can now learn to cater for your deeper needs without having to be sick or having to start feeling guilty that you have made yourself sick. It gives you a means to create better health for yourself, which frequently can determine the course of your life.

The advantages of the usual system, whereby you believe that you are not in any way responsible for any illness, are that it exonerates you from all responsibility for getting sick and harming your body, it covers up your fears, and it gives you a way of fulfilling your needs. The only trouble is that it also leaves you powerless, unsatisfied and, above all, sick!

Our intuition is a powerful tool in dealing with the body's needs and one which, as we have seen, is frequently under-used. We should learn to listen to our intuition more. A good way to do this is to practise it. For instance, first thing in the morning, before you get out of bed, just lie quietly and ask yourself something about the day. For example, if you happen to be a receptionist you can wonder about the number of people who are going to pass before your desk that day. You may be a secretary, in which case ask yourself how many letters you may have to type that day. Listen for the answer and then during the day see if your intuition was right. If you were, check back to the way you felt at the time. If you were not right, check back again. Note the difference. Gradually you can start to use the feedback to develop and gain confidence in your own powers. You will be amazed how quickly you can train your intuition and how often you will find that you are right.

Another important exercise is to find time during the day to be quiet and go inside yourself. This isn't always easy in our busy lives, but do try to make some time, however short it may be. Perhaps it will mean locking yourself in the bathroom for ten minutes, but that is better than nothing! Once there, think about one of the day's problems and ask your intuition what you should do about it. Listen carefully for the answer and as the day goes on see just how good an answer it was. Gradually you can learn to ask bigger and bigger questions and learn to rely more and more on the answers you receive.

Once you have developed this skill you should then make a point of asking yourself certain questions. One of them is 'What do I need to make myself totally healthy?' First of all ask what your body needs, and then what your soul needs. Ignore the little gremlin who tries to tempt you with chocolate and cheesecake; try to concentrate on deeper and more meaningful matters. Your intuition *is* powerful. If it tells you that something or someone is bad for you, then it is, and if it tells you something is good for you, then it is. But if you are trying hard to convince yourself that something or someone is good for you, but your inner intuition keeps telling you that it's really bad, then be assured it's bad!

Let's try a small exercise now to see how well honed your intuition is. Close your eyes and relax. Reach quietly inside yourself and deliberate on a question about your health. Listen to your intuition and what it tells you. Your questions can be something like these:

Is coffee good for me?
Should I take more exercise?
Do I eat too many sweets?
Do I drink too much?
Do I rest enough?

Make up your own list of health-related questions, write the answers down on a piece of paper and keep it in your wallet. As the days go by see how correct your intuition was.

In the earlier chapters we looked at reasons *why* you might be sabotaging your health consciously or subconsciously. To end this chapter let's look at the various ways you might be doing it.

Firstly, list all the things you do to your body that you know, or suspect, are bad for you. Be honest — after all, no one but you need ever read the list. Now make another list of all the other things you do that you have even the slightest doubts about. Your lists might include such things as drinking too much alcohol, eating sugar, not taking any exercise, eating on the run, not relaxing, smoking, working too hard or not sleeping properly.

Secondly, beside each item on your list write *why* you do it and what benefits you could be getting from it. Your list may now begin to look something like this:

I drink too much alcohol. . .
    It helps me unwind with my friends.
I work too hard. . .
    I am avoiding facing an empty marriage.

Thirdly, write down at least three ways of dealing with each of these situations. For instance, you could relax with your friends at the theatre, or play tennis or bush-walk. If it is an empty marriage you are avoiding facing up to, you could actually face up to it fair and square and try to improve it.

In the long run the outcome is much more likely to be satisfactory than if you hide behind drugs and superficial cover-ups.

# MECHANICS FOR BEGINNERS

So far we have seen that there are many things that have influenced the development of our belief patterns. They will influence our approach to life and the decisions that we make. Not only are our mental attitudes affected but our bodies are, too. Our thoughts affect the way our body works. But exactly how does this occur? Let's take a little trip inside the body and see what happens. To understand this complicated system better, we will present it in a simplified cartoon form.

The first thing we encounter during our journey through the human body is the nervous system. Looking rather like a map of the London underground system, the nervous system radiates out through the entire body, operated from the central switchboard (the brain) by two controllers who manage the two branches of the autonomic nervous system: Simon the Sympathetic and Peter the Parasympathetic. Via the physical senses, the sympathetic nervous system reacts to hidden dangers and life-threatening events. When the little bleeps started on his control-room screen, Simon would summon up Archie Adrenalin, who would start the pump going and send his valuable liquid racing through the veins. Once the system was full, Simon and Archie would report to Peter, who all along had been getting on with the work of directing the internal housekeeping, and tell him to stop work until the emergency was over. Sometimes Simon would decide to stand and fight, but at others times, deciding that discretion was the better part of valour, he would decide to flee. 'Fight or Flight' Simon they quickly dubbed him, but no-one could deny that he was able to make decisions in the twinkling of an eye, and generally the right ones at that.

However, as time wore on and the jungle started to clear a bit, Simon's role became less and less necessary. Times and behaviour had changed and the rest of the tribe took it very badly if Simon made the wrong decision and decided to run away when the parking meter man started writing out a ticket. It was worse still when he decided, as he sometimes did, to stand and fight and persuaded you to end up thumping the fellow, who after all was only doing his duty. It was just that Simon's role was no longer appropriate to the times and he was retired on half pay to sit in a comfy chair all day, keeping a weather eye on the controls but not having to do too much work.

Inevitably Simon got bored and dreamed up a little game for himself which he called, for want of a better name, Stress. The idea of the game was to take an event and see how uncomfortable he could make you feel about it. Sometimes he would be very successful and when you got really uncomfortable he would sing out 'Stressed!' in a loud, shrill voice rather like a demented bridge player with a Grand Slam. On those occasions he would reckon he had won the hand. But on other occasions he would not succeed in getting you worked up and he would have to settle for defeat, allowing Peter to smile complacently and get on with his duties.

To help him in this sadistic little ritual, Simon enrolled the help of Harry Hypothalamus. Harry lived in a comfortable little niche in the front of the brain and spent a lot of time either laughing or crying, depending on the weather and what was going on around him. He was a very emotional chap was Harry, and everyone was in awe of him. Always slightly afraid of going out alone, Harry had formed his own support chain which he rather grandly called The Hypothalamic Pituitary Adreno-Cortical Axis! The HPACA had quite strict guidelines laid down for its behaviour and Harry had dictated exactly what everyone was to do in the event of any emergency. The rules he laid down went something like this:

On receiving the command from Brigadier Brain's messengers, who are known in the dark world of the skull as 'Thoughts', Harry Hypothalamus would pass along to Paul Pituitary a special substance called a hormone. On receiving this hormone, Paul would unleash his dog, called ACTH, who would immediately descend to the kidney zone and bite Anthony Adrenal-Cortex, who by this time was getting rather fed up with the whole system. However, being the good, well-educated fellow that his name suggests, Adrenal-Cortex would immediately upon being bitten ring up Archie Adrenalin and Charlie Cortisone and tell them to start running like hell. All the little Archies and Charlies would immediately take off for the target tissues to which they had been directed, homing in like a Sidewinder missile fired from a jet fighter. In no time at all they would start attaching themselves to various parts of the human body, with all the tenacity of a Crown of Thorns starfish on the Great Barrier Reef, throwing everything into the fray with not a thought for tomorrow. Some would see to it that the kidneys pumped out more hormones and created higher blood pressure. He, he, that was always a popular one! Or they would set about atrophying the lymph nodes or shrinking the thymus, both common pranks which gave them great satisfaction. Others would set about damaging the artery walls to see if they could succeed in creating the disease known to man as atherosclerosis. In short, they had become a pretty ghastly bunch whose roles had become largely outdated and could quite easily make you feel like a Mexican in the path of The Magnificent Seven in a world where physically fighting or fleeing are no longer acceptable ways of dealing with most challenges.

Thus it can be seen that the mechanism exists within your body for thoughts, feelings and reactions to outside events to affect the chemistry and function of the different parts of your body.

Yes, but where, you might ask, does this get us with regard to our *health*? Well, the answer is that it gets us a long way. We've just seen that our bodies will react to outside influences, and to inside influences (our thoughts), too. This being the case, does it not therefore follow that we can think ourselves ill? And if we can think ourselves ill, then surely we can think ourselves well again?

You don't believe it? Then ask yourself this question: when was the last time you felt acutely embarrassed in front of other people? Just remember that time for a moment. Have you just blushed? Many people would and the reason for that is simple. The mere act of thinking that thought, in this case 'What a fool I was!', was sufficient for the blood vessels in your face to dilate and contract, forcing blood into the face and causing you to go red. So you see you can change the whole physiology of your body for a certain length of time just by a thought! The thought gives rise to an emotion of some sort (embarrassment, anger, anxiety, happiness), which in turn affects the sympathetic and parasympathetic nervous systems and thus the body function and chemistry.

And it isn't such a big leap from our thoughts changing our physiology in blushing to our thoughts changing our bodies in such a way as to create serious health problems. Nerves and fear can lead to palpitations, while emotional upset can lead to asthma. More sustained thoughts and emotions can have cumulative long-term implications.

There are a number of very common complaints which people often give themselves and will most probably admit to being responsible for. They include headaches, ulcers, diarrhoea and even grey hair. The cause of these complaints is often self-induced. For example, if you worry and fret a lot over something you can give yourself a headache. Basically, your thoughts have given you this headache — you have given yourself the headache. The headache has come from your thoughts about the situation and the stress that you feel you are under because of it. On top of giving himself headaches, the busy executive might also give himself ulcers. He's always on the go, rushing here and there, too busy to eat properly, and when he does sit down to eat, his thoughts are on what he must do as soon as the meal is over. The result is that he lets his thoughts, and the resulting stress and anxiety, adversely affect his digestive system, and in no time at all he has given himself an ulcer. He then invariably compounds the problem by believing that he is a one-ulcer man holding down a two-ulcer job and that only aggravates the situation!

There are many people who find it a most frightening experience to have to stand up in front of a crowd of people and address them. Stage fright like this can often express itself in the form of diarrhoea or repeated trips to the toilet before the event. In effect the nervous thoughts about the coming event have created a reaction in the body. A great many well-known actors suffer terribly from stage fright, but as they will tell you, it doesn't matter whether they are suffering from fright, a migraine or any other complaint, the show must go on. So when they get on stage with their thoughts focused on the audience, everything else is put aside for their performance. Back in the wings they start to think of themselves again and relapse into their fright or pain once more. It's another example of mind over matter. The same thing can cause grey hair. There are a great many well documented cases of people whose hair has quite literally turned grey (or white) overnight as the result of some particular pressure or great emotional trauma. It's just another example of how the body will react to emotional stimuli.

It is actually possible to gain complete control over your body and this can be aided by using the technique of bio-feedback. This is a simple system whereby you can measure particular responses that your body gives to certain stimuli on a special machine and 'think' them down. As you think down a pain in the finger, for example, you will hear the tone on the feedback machine actually lower. By concentrating on that tone you can think the pain away altogether.

The yogis of India have perfected this art to such a degree that they don't need machines to help them. A great many other people around the world have also learnt how to control aspects of their body so as to improve their general health. It has been proved possible, for example, to slow the heartbeat right down and reduce brain waves from the usual 14–28 cycles (or Beta waves), down to 8–13 cycles (or Alpha waves), or even as low as 4–7 cycles (or Theta waves), in some advanced instances. Yogis can also alter their skin temperature in selected parts of the body, so much so that an advanced yogi can turn the left half of the palm of his hand bright red and tingly whilst the right-hand side is grey and deathly cold — but that's a state which you're only likely to reach if you're prepared to sit on a mountain top and contemplate your navel for the rest of your life!

There are plenty of stories of people who have been able consciously to slow their pulse rate down so much that they can stay buried alive for great lengths of time where the ordinary person would have died from lack of oxygen. And of course we've all heard stories of men and women walking over burning coals without feeling any pain or suffering from blistered feet later. A favourite nightclub act in the Middle East is for a fakir to stick knives and pins through sensitive parts of his body, such as his tongue or his fingers, without drawing any blood. That's just another example of how the mind can control the body.

This being so, it must be plausible to suggest that we can create illness, either consciously or subconsciously, with our thoughts and our emotions? If we can create illness, then surely we can just as easily heal ourselves?

It has been proved that it is actually possible to wall yourself off from illness and disease. In their book *Getting Well Again*, Carl Simonton and Stephanie Matthews-Simonton quote an American study which provided an extreme example of this by using two groups of schizophrenics. One was a group of catatonic schizophrenics, people who had apparently shut themselves off from the world and whose brain had apparently closed down, and the other was a group of paranoid schizophrenics, people who suffered actively from a variety of delusions. It was shown that the catatonic schizophrenics, the ones who had shut themselves off from the world, had fewer instances of cancer than the general population, whereas the paranoid schizophrenics showed a higher rate than the national average. [1]

So you see, our thoughts can control how our body functions. This means that we can choose to control our bodies for better health. By closing the mind down to certain stimuli it is possible to shut certain things effectively out of your body, including even the most life-threatening diseases.

CHAPTER   10
# LETTING GO OF FEAR, ANGER AND STRESS

We've seen from examples in the previous chapter that emotional tension can change our body chemistry. If it can change body chemistry, then it can change your health. For example, emotional tension leads to physical tension, which in turn leads to constriction of the blood vessels which can result in high blood pressure or, in the worst cases, a stroke.

While any emotion can affect the body's chemistry, it is negative emotion that, naturally, produces negative effects. Two of the most devastating are fear and anger. There must be few of us who haven't felt these emotions at some stage in our lives. In fact there are a great many people who, for different reasons, spend most of their waking hours enveloped in one or other of them.

But before we look at the root causes of fear and anger, let's consider briefly their physical manifestations. Fear usually starts as an impulse in the brain. It is a reaction to a particular stimulus, such as suddenly realising that you are sharing your picnic with a three-metre long black snake or that your lover has made a secret date to see someone else next Tuesday lunchtime. The outward manifestation of fear is often an increased sensation of sensitivity in the skin, sweating palms, a dry mouth, rapid breathing and a heart that has just beaten a Formula One driver round a Grand Prix circuit.

Often accompanying these symptoms will be a sinking feeling in the stomach, and a dread awareness that something ghastly is about to unfold before you. What is happening, in fact, is that your sympathetic nervous system is manufacturing adrenalin and pumping it through your body by the bucketful. While this is happening your nervous system is desperately trying to make up its mind what to do next. If you have ever been rabbit shooting you will know that the first thing a bunny will do when it hears you approach is sit up and prick its ears. It will sense you and temporarily 'freeze' before racing off for shelter. This temporary 'freezing' is the sympathetic nervous system manufacturing adrenalin and preparing the animal to either fight or flee. How many bad paperback novels have you read which contain sentences like this: 'The door slowly creaked open. Jim quickly turned, but what he saw left him frozen in horror' or words to that effect? Fight or flight is the natural response of any animal, big or small, to impending danger. The decision is made by the involuntary nervous system picking up the danger signals, manufacturing adrenalin, and then passing the information along to the voluntary nervous system which will make the decision as to what to do about the situation.

While short-term reactions to emotions such as fear and anger may do no harm, sustained emotional pressure can affect your health. For example, if you experience fear over a long period, the inevitable increase of adrenalin in your body will adversely affect the heart and other organs.

Many emotions which you experience result in an increase of thyroxin in the body, which in turn leads to altered metabolic rates and can affect your weight, physical appearance and levels of activity and energy. Pain can result in the release of substances called endorphins in the brain and pituitary gland which will determine just how much pain we can tolerate. Endorphins are the body's own pain-killers and are produced automatically -- up to a point. This explains the delay in the experience or development of pain during the first (shock) phase of an accident. If we could develop greater conscious control over production, it is possible that we could significantly increase our pain tolerance, and thus reduce the need for pain-killing drugs with their adverse side effects. It must be remembered, however, that pain serves as an important warning signal and should not be blocked out indiscriminately.

It is fascinating to note here in passing that a man who had been hospitalised with severe connective tissue disorder and was in a great deal of pain managed to maintain himself in a tolerable state of comfort through laughter. He played the funniest films he knew throughout the day on a video screen and discovered that ten minutes of good belly laughter manufactured sufficient endorphins to keep him free of pain for almost two hours.

Anger and anxiety will affect you by switching on the sympathetic nervous system which, in turn, will cause the parasympathetic nervous system to be turned off. This will result, among other things, in decreased digestive activity. The result therefore of prolonged anger or anxiety can be such digestive diseases as ulcers or colitis.

The division of feeling between fear and anger is only slight. Many of the same symptoms are present in both emotions and frequently anger can be brought about by fear. Whereas fear is a much more primitive emotion, built in to animal consciousness as a protective measure, anger is a second order emotion usually triggered by other primary causes. A typical example of anger caused by fear would be discovering that your loved one was having an affair with someone else. The anger in this case would be brought on by the primary fear that you were in danger of losing the person you loved, as well as by a sense of betrayal and loss of face.

Anger can also be brought on by frustration. Once again, although the emotion is triggered by an outside source, it is also often triggered by the internal feeling of one's own inadequacy. For example, knowing that you are unable to complete a work assignment because you do not have sufficient knowledge to do so, you rail at the employer who set you the task. You claim it to be a stupid waste of your time and the man in question to be an idiot for thinking up the task in the first place.

Fear and anger have one thing in common. They can both make you ill. You've heard the expression 'I was sick with fear'. It's not strictly accurate. A more literal translation would be 'I was so afraid I subconsciously (or consciously!) made myself sick'. Illness is a tool which we humans can conveniently and cleverly bend to our service to cover up a multitude of unpleasant events which we don't want to face. It is much safer to be sick than to be exposed as inadequate in any situation so, very sensibly, we often choose the former.

People who are often afraid are also often ill and exhausted. The next time you feel really emotionally washed out ask yourself the question 'What is it that I am afraid of at this moment?' It might be that you are afraid of losing someone, or of not being loved. Maybe it's the fear that you won't get your own way, or that you may have to do something unpleasant. It could be that you are afraid that you will lose your money, or it may simply be the fear that you will not be taken care of. Whatever it is, it is making you sick — literally sick with fear.

However, since we now recognise that we actually create our own sickness and our own health, we can also recognise that we might create situations to cope with an upcoming unpleasantness. For example, you know that the boss is going to call you in tomorrow morning and give you a dressing-down for some misdemeanour, so you develop a bad cold or a migraine and have to stay in bed that day rather than go to work. The 'decision' may well take place below the level of consciousness. Huge amounts of energy will be spent in burying your fear, pushing it to the back of your mind and finding reasons for not facing up to it. In other words, you simply feel scared, but, in succumbing to the fear, your adrenal glands are affected. This in turn dampens your immune system and hence you develop a cold. Your secondary emotion will probably come into play as well when you are pushed and you will get angry when challenged to do something about it. If you can deal with your fear you may, consciously or subconsciously, avoid the cold.

Stop right now and list some of the things of which you are afraid at this moment. Be absolutely honest with yourself. Then beside each one write down how you are coping with it. How is your health at this moment?

Now we challenge you to do something positive about your fears. How do you feel? Do you feel angry because you can't think of anything you are frightened of although you feel that there must be something? Or do you feel angry that you don't know what to do about it? Do you feel angry at having your fears exposed? Has your mind just gone blank?

Don't worry, you're in the 100 per cent of people who feel exactly the same way! It may help to realise that by making yourself ill you have found a way to fulfil a certain need. You are in fact not sick at all, merely in need, which is quite a different kettle of fish. You can actually be quite proud of having found a way to fulfil that need, but realise that there are other, more pleasant, cures that do not compromise your physical health.

There are seven steps forward which you might care to take at this stage.

Be prepared to take responsibility for yourself.
Be prepared to take some risks.
Learn to understand why you have created your illness.
Determine the benefits you derive from it.
Decide whether or not you can do without the illness.
Find alternative ways of establishing the life you want
　　for yourself and caring for your needs.
Learn to love yourself.

When the body starts to become sick it is a sign that your coping mechanisms are breaking down. Whether it is a major or a minor illness you may be experiencing or have just experienced, the chances are that it was preceded by a period of feeling run down and overstressed. You may have been feeling short-changed in the love and care department and in need of help which wasn't forthcoming. You may have had to deprive yourself of sufficient rest and relaxation and allowed yourself to become undernourished, of either food or love. The chances are that throughout all this you were steadfastly trying to maintain your normal behaviour beliefs or patterns which in fact were stifling your real needs.

It is important to assess your thoughts, attitudes, feelings and behaviour at the different stages in your life. How are they when you are feeling well? What changes do they undergo just before you get sick? And how are they when you are sick?

Fear and anger often lie at the root of sickness and ill-health. The events in your life anything up to eighteen months prior to an illness (and sometimes even longer) can be a useful guide in determining why you have become ill. However, it is not the event itself but the way you choose to respond to it that determines the effect. Try this exercise now. Do it before reading the next paragraph. Get a piece of paper and a pen and spend just two minutes writing down how you would feel if your partner, or if you haven't got a partner, your closest friend, were to leave you today. What would you do about it?

Did you see your partner's departure as a rejection of you? Or did you see it as a challenge? Did it perhaps prod you to re-evaluate yourself and re-examine your behaviour and attitudes? Or was it an opportunity to get out and meet new people? Did you see it as an opportunity to develop some new friends or hobbies that you didn't have time for before? Or was it just the beginning of loneliness? The interpretation you choose to put on it depends entirely on your own value and estimation of yourself. It may very well be that your partner leaving you had absolutely nothing whatsoever to do with you. They may have felt they needed a change, or perhaps they were going through a mid-life crisis, or they may even have felt that you were about to leave them and thought they'd better get in first! How you interpreted this action says much for your own strength and independence, and much more about you than about them. Think about the way you have developed, about your interest in other people, and the extent of your own interests and hobbies. All these things have a bearing on your attitudes and on how you will stand up to the emotional challenge posed above.

If you are prepared to explore the limitations that you place on yourself you can create new and wider areas of growth and fulfilment. Seemingly negative situations can be quickly turned into positive ones and you can do away with the need to be ill as an answer for getting what you want. In short, you can create exactly what you want without having to resort to the sympathy of others.

Let's try another exercise. Think of a time when you had a serious illness. (If you can't think of one in the last two years then give yourself a big pat on the back!) Now write down the six events that most affected your life in the six months preceding the illness. Look at physical, mental and emotional events, internal and external causes and lastly, the amount of care, or lack of care, that you were giving yourself and others at the time. The chances are that prior to your illness there were quite a few worries which you have now listed on your sheet of paper. Take a moment to understand the relationship between the two and determine how the various stresses could have affected your health.

Now let's see if you can do exactly the same thing to *prevent* an illness. Write down the six major worries in your life at the moment. Once you have done that, see if you can think of another way of looking at them. Can they be removed altogether or is there a way to reinterpret them? For example, work is hell at the moment and everyone hates the boss. You dread going to the office each morning. What can you do about it? Well, one way to deal with the situation is to make yourself ill. That way you have a perfect excuse for not having to go to work and face the unpleasantness. But isn't that rather a drastic answer? After all, there are plenty of good parts in the day that you want to enjoy, so why ruin the whole of it for just a small part?

The other answer is to re-examine the problem. The boss is rude and arrogant and makes everyone's life a misery. First of all make up your mind that, whatever happens, you are not going to allow yourself to be affected by his/her behaviour. After all, the worst thing that can happen to you is that you get the sack and that is scarcely a life-threatening state of affairs! As well, make the decision that however nasty the boss is to you, you are going to be sweetness and light personified back. You may be amazed at the result. We recommended this approach to a young girl who was having problems with her very difficult boss in an insurance office. Within a fortnight she was offered the job as the man's personal secretary and now the two of them get on just fine. He is a lot nicer to the rest of the staff too!

More often than not a re-examination and reinterpretation of those events in your life which have caused you to feel afraid or angry can lead to a whole new approach. In so doing you remove the necessity to make yourself ill as a solution to the problem.

You will notice that so far we have avoided using the word 'stress'. It is a word we hear constantly. Whole forests have been cut down so that books, learned papers and not so learned magazine articles can be written about it. And it is possibly the most life-threatening force we encounter on a daily basis.

So what is stress? Is it a chemical that gets into the brain? Is it a clamp that restricts the blood vessels? Is it a virus? No, it's none of these things. In fact there is no such independent entity as 'stress'. Stress is *caused*. It is a result of *your* response to a situation. It is a state of severe tension that is brought on when we find ourselves under a lot of psychological or physical pressure (or both). You can feel stressed when you are under some sort of emotional strain (particularly those two dread emotions, fear and anger), for example you may be very concerned about relationship problems or a sick child. You might also become stressed when you are pushing your mind and body to the limit, such as when you have to meet some sort of deadline for work or study for an exam. Obviously, as we have seen, this can have profound effects on the state of our mental and physical well-being.

There are all sorts of outside events which we perceive as being 'stressful', but we can actually stop any of them being harmful to us if we can change our attitudes towards them. In effect you only become stressed if you allow it to happen.

Let's take an example. You are driving along in your car when someone behind you starts honking their horn aggressively and tries to overtake. They succeed, and as they pass they make a rude gesture and then speed off into the distance. You are left to react in one of two ways. You can either sit there calmly and think: 'What a stupid, rude, aggressive person. I can only imagine that they have just had a terrible experience and are very upset.' That's the saint-like approach and results in absolutely no stress to your system at all. Alternatively you can react like 90 per cent of the population and become very annoyed. As soon as the honking starts you feel a knot in the stomach and by the time the aggressive driver is alongside your car you are mouthing obscenities at him (strangely enough women rarely seem to release their aggression in this particular manner!) and making rude gestures back. In short you have just bought in to his problem and in so doing you have raised your own stress level significantly. You have allowed his stress to become your stress quite unnecessarily. So you see, by understanding how stress can develop you can avoid it.

It is recognised by the majority of medical practitioners that certain factors in life will produce stressful responses in the majority of people and that if too many of these factors come together at once then a person may become ill. This is now understandable, since we have seen how it is possible to make ourselves ill just by thinking. Dr

Thomas H. Holmes, Dr Rahe and their associates at the University of Washington School of Medicine isolated the most common of these stress factors and gave them a value based on their observations of the correlation between the factors and the resulting physical illness. People were then asked to evaluate their score which could in turn be related to their patterns of illness or their likelihood of becoming ill in the future.[1]

Before telling you how the test is scored, here is the scale which they came up with. Do it yourself and see what score you get. Mark it twice, first on the basis of events which have happened to you in the past twelve months, and second on the basis of the most stressful year of your life that you can remember.

## STRESS RATING SCALE

| EVENT | SCORE |
|---|---|
| Death of spouse | 100 |
| Divorce | 73 |
| Marital separation | 65 |
| Jail term | 63 |
| Death of close family member | 63 |
| Personal injury or illness | 53 |
| Marriage | 50 |
| Fired from work | 47 |
| Marital reconciliation | 45 |
| Retirement | 45 |
| Change in family member's health | 44 |
| Pregnancy | 39 |
| Sex difficulties | 39 |
| Addition to family | 39 |
| Business readjustments | 39 |
| Change in financial status | 38 |
| Death of close friend | 37 |
| Change to different line of work | 36 |

| | |
|---|---|
| Change in number of marital arguments | 36 |
| Mortgage or loan over $10,000 | 31 |
| Foreclosure of mortgage or loan | 30 |
| Change in work responsibilities | 29 |
| Son or daughter leaving home | 29 |
| Trouble with in-laws | 29 |
| Outstanding personal achievement | 28 |
| Spouse begins or stops work | 26 |
| Starting or finishing school, college, etc. | 26 |
| Change in living conditions | 25 |
| Revision of personal habits | 24 |
| Trouble with the boss | 23 |
| Change in work hours, conditions | 20 |
| Change in residence | 20 |
| Change in schools | 20 |
| Change in recreational habits | 19 |
| Change in church activities | 18 |
| Mortgage or loan under $10,000 | 17 |
| Change in sleep habits | 16 |
| Change in number of family gatherings | 15 |
| Change in eating habits | 15 |
| Holidays | 13 |
| Christmas season | 12 |
| Minor violation of the law | 11 |

As you can see, not all of the entries in the above list are negative events, but even positive ones can be perceived as stressful if the intensity is great enough.

Now to the scoring. In the study done originally in Washington, the doctors found that 49 per cent of people who scored more than 300 in the chosen twelve month period reported illness during that period. Nine per cent of people who scored less than 200 during the period also reported some illness, and people who scored in the top 33 per cent had 90 per cent more illness than people who scored in the bottom 33 per cent of the study. Of course we must point out that 51 per cent of those who scored more than 300 got no illness, which points to the fact that they must have perceived these 'stresses' in a different light.

A neat definition of illness is that it is distorted thought in a physical form. If we allow our thoughts about a particular matter to shift out of focus, then we can make ourselves ill. We can, however, equally choose not to be ill by not allowing the particular event to worry us to that degree. The choice is now yours.

Like other creative thoughts and reactions, stress is also dealt with in part by the body's sympathetic nervous system. This system copes with the pressures of the outside world and, as we said earlier, controls our 'fight or flight' mechanism and our bodily functions. Imagine, for example, that you are walking through a field when all of a sudden you hear a fearful bellowing and turn to see a huge black bull bearing down on you with all the speed and ferocity of the Light Brigade. Your immediate reaction, thanks to the sympathetic nervous system, is to run like hell! While you are running, the sympathetic nervous system cleverly stops your body processing any food it may have in there and blocks off your exhaust tubes. After all, you're not going to last long if you have to stop to go to the toilet! To take the analogy further, occasions of extreme and long-term stress can cause the parasympathetic nervous system to shut down and thus stop your digestive processes which can, if this lasts long enough, lead to a variety of illnesses connected with the stomach or the intestines.

Further, an unpleasant effect of chronic stress is that it plays havoc with the body's natural immune system. The actions of the hypothalamus and pituitary (and ACTH), all part of the hypothalamic adreno-cortical axis, cause constant flooding of adrenalin, cortisone and other hormones into the bloodstream. The immune system becomes depressed as a result of this, and there is an immediate increased risk of infection and disease. Such diseases can be quite minor, like a cold in the head, or quite major, like cancer.

Another form of stress which is quite common among human beings and quite inevitable is bereavement. When we lose someone whom we loved and cared for, we feel very sad and go through a period of depression. Dr R. W. Bathrop of New South Wales University conducted a test on twenty-six bereaved men and women to find out just how their systems were affected by the death of a loved one. The participants were tested at two weeks and again at six weeks after the death of their spouse. Dr Bathrop found that in all of them the lymphocyte function was significantly depressed. What this means in layman's terms is that there were significantly fewer white cells in the blood and these are needed for the destruction of disease-producing micro-organisms. In other words, sad or stressed people are more likely to become ill than are happy people.

Major work into the connection between severe emotional stress and cancer has been done in the United States by oncologist Dr Carl Simonton and his psychotherapist wife, Stephanie Matthews-Simonton. After years of studying cancer patients at their centre in Dallas, Texas, they have come to the conclusion that the link between stress and illness is so clear that it is now possible to predict illness based on the amount of perceived stress in a person's life, and conversely to eradicate it by dealing with these perceived stresses in a new and more positive way.

This is by no means a new idea. Professor Hans Selye of the University of Prague first formulated such a theory in the 1920s. He later moved to Canada and became the director of the Institute of Experimental Medicine and Surgery at the University of Montreal. His studies there quite clearly showed the adverse effects of stress on the body, resulting in chronic hormonal imbalances which can lead to a range of life-threatening conditions. Selye's research showed that the bodily reaction to stress produced exactly the right conditions for abnormal cells to flourish and it came as no surprise to the Simontons to find that a great majority of cancer sufferers have in fact got a severely depressed immune system brought about by stress.

The sympathetic nervous system will also process perceived stressful events of a less dramatic nature unless you are prepared to take over the controls and stop flying on automatic.

There are a number of different ways in which stress can be relieved and whole books have been written on this subject. Here are just a few simple methods to be going on with:

Laughter is a great stress reducer

Stroking the body reduces blood pressure (so does stroking the dog!)

Anger should be expressed at once rather than hung on to

Don't carry one stressful situation through to another

Visualisation of a problem can often help the brain to manufacture a cure

Listen to your favourite music

Stand on a mountain top or sit in your car with the windows up and the radio at full blast and shout your lungs out

As previously mentioned, studies that have been done with bio-feedback have clearly shown that it is possible to 'think down' a problem. If there is a particular event which is causing you stress, go away into a quiet corner, close your eyes and think it through calmly. As you do this you will gradually dispel the stressful elements of the event and come up with an answer. It is important that you organise some method for coping with, or defusing, stress because any sort of prolonged emotional tension will ultimately create physical tension. In other words, sooner or later you are going to make yourself ill.

Very often stress is something which can be cured by simple organisation techniques. It may just be a matter of rearranging your timetable, or keeping out of a particular person's way. If that is the case, then don't punish yourself unnecessarily by refusing to make the necessary changes. If these changes are, for some reason, impossible to make, then acknowledge what is in store for you and refuse to allow it to stress you. Using the technique we discussed in an earlier chapter, work out why a particular event or person is causing you this stress. Often you will find that it is not really your problem at all and then you can stop worrying about it altogether. Alternatively go to the heart of the matter.

Take the case of Mary D. Her boss insisted on explaining every new task to her in the minutest detail and every time he did this she became angry. It got to the stage where she dreaded anything new, any change in the routine. After seeking advice about her reaction, Mary was asked to complete the following statements:

The reason my boss's explanations make me cross is. . . 'they irritate me'

The reason they irritate me is. . .'he thinks I couldn't work them out for myself.'

He thinks I couldn't work it out for myself because. . .'he thinks I'm stupid'

He thinks I'm stupid because. . .'everyone thinks I'm stupid'

Everyone thinks I'm stupid because... 'I am stupid'

The first person to think I was stupid was... 'my older brothers'

Bingo, there we have it! Her older brothers, from the arrogance of their three and five year advantages, had spent their childhood telling their younger sister that she was stupid for not being as advanced as them and not being able to keep up with them. From then on Mary, having understood that, was able to disassociate her boss's explanations from her childhood feeling of inadequacy and to appreciate his assistance and support.

# PAIN — HOW TO BEAR THE UNBEARABLE

One of the elements of life with which we all have to con-
tend at some time or another is pain. Whether it be a bad
headache or an abscess on the tooth or just hitting our
thumb with a hammer while hanging a picture, pain is a
common part of everyday life.

There are generally two normal attitudes to pain. You
can either grit your teeth and bear it, or you can break
down and shriek and scream and jump around waving the
offending limb like the lead guitarist at a pop concert.
There is, however, a third method, which is not normally
used. You can actually control pain with the power of your
mind. In reality you do it practically every day of your life
without being aware of it. Think back and remember a
time when you were having such fun that you were not
aware that you had hurt yourself until some time later. It's
happened to nearly everyone at some stage in their lives.

To illustrate the point, let us tell you about a riding
accident that Xandria had some years ago. Together with

a group of friends she was out on a bush trail on an all-day riding expedition. It was a fun day, the weather was warm without being too hot, and everyone was having a great time. Pushing the horses into a gentle canter, the party made their way along the side of the mountain with Xandria bringing up the rear. Not as experienced as the others, she was a little nervous but nevertheless determined to keep up. Suddenly the trail took a sharp left-hand bend and without warning Xandria found herself caught up in a low hanging branch. The horse carried on at full canter and it was all Xandria could do to stay in the saddle, but she retained her seat and was mighty proud of herself for doing so. Half an hour or so later, the party came to a halt in a clearing and decided to stop for lunch. It was then that someone noticed the deep gash along the side of Xandria's mouth. Without wanting to alarm her, he gently brought the wound to her attention and then, for the very first time, she felt the tremendous pain the gash was causing her. Without further ado she was whisked to hospital and had eight stitches inserted in the side of her mouth.

As long as her mind was preoccupied with something else, in this case trying to keep up with the party and stay in the saddle, there was no time to dwell on the pain of the accident. But as soon as that preoccupation was over and she had time to dwell on the pain, then it quickly became unbearable.

Another good example is the pain that many people experience when they go to the dentist. What with novo-caine, laughing gas and other modern inventions, dentistry is not nearly as painful as it used to be twenty or thirty years ago, and certainly the days of anaesthetising the patient with a bottle of whisky are long past. However, many people still dread a visit to the dentist and even the smallest injection can cause them great pain. The reason, of course, is that the mind is preparing for that pain long before the visit even happens. It doesn't matter what precautions the dentist takes, you are going to feel pain.

Enlightened dentists have realised for some years now the importance of taking the patient's mind off what is going on in their mouth and all sorts of gimmicks have popped up in dental surgeries lately. A cageful of budgerigars is a popular one, and running commentaries from the dentist on the state of play in the latest cricket test match make some people wonder whether they haven't come to the hairdresser by mistake! One dentist of our acquaintance has overcome the pain problem in a number of effective ways. Firstly he has a huge mirror hung at an angle over the chair so that the recumbent patient can watch the activity in the street nine floors below. Secondly, upon seating the patient in the chair he offers a menu of either popular or classical music which can be listened to through a small pair of headphones or, alternatively, a selection of video tapes which can be viewed on a screen mounted on the wall above the chair. This latter ploy is remarkably effective.

It has been recognised for thousands of years that one human sense can be used to overcome another. There is an old Chinese proverb which loosely translated says 'The best way to cure a headache is to cut off your arm'. Basically what that means is that the greater pain of losing the arm will quickly make you forget about the minor pain in your head. In a rather less drastic way, in activating the sense of hearing by having sound pumped directly into your eardrums at a sufficiently loud volume, you can lessen the awareness of the pain being experienced in another part of the body. The greater the pain, the louder the music. This is a very effective cure for such things as sinus pains, assorted headaches, toothache, and aches and pains in other regions of the body.

There can be no doubt that pain is also exacerbated by anxiety. The more worried you become about a particular pain, the worse that pain will seem. Likewise, the more pain we feel, the more distressed we become. In such cases the first thing to do is to put ourselves into a more positive and less distressed frame of mind and this can be done by practising a variety of relaxing mental exercises. To achieve this we must first relax physically. It is very hard to become mentally relaxed if our bodies are as tight as a coiled cobra waiting to strike.

The principles of mental and physical relaxation are similar to those of creative visualisation which we looked at in an earlier chapter. To create physical relaxation, first close your eyes and talk to your body. It's not a bad idea to make a tape which you can play at such times. It would go something like this:

Feel your feet and your toes, be aware of them and feel them relax. (Pause) Now feel your legs up to your knees, feel them relax and feel the tension draining out of them. (Pause) Now feel your thighs and feel them relax. (Pause) Be aware of your groin and feel any tension draining out of it. (Pause) Now feel your stomach and feel it settle gently. (Pause) Move up to your chest and be aware of your breathing. Listen to your breathing and feel relaxed. (Pause) Now feel the tension in your back, your shoulders and your neck and feel that tension slowly draining down your arms and out through your fingers. (Pause) Lastly feel your face and your head and let all the muscles in your face relax and feel completely at peace. (Pause) You are now completely relaxed.

The commands should of course be spoken in a gentle, soothing voice and you can accompany them with some soft background music. What you now have is a very useful tape which you can carry around with you and use at moments of high tension, such as before important business meetings or visits to the dentist. You can even play it on your (or his) portable tape-recorder when you are sitting in that dreaded chair!

Once you have induced a state of physical relaxation in this manner you can set about visualising, or conjuring up for yourself, mental images which will combat the pain you may be feeling in some part of the body. The combination of a perfectly relaxed body and a powerful positive mental image will work wonders.

As we have clearly seen the introduction of pleasurable stimuli can quickly overcome any reasonable painful experience. Any mother will confirm this. Many is the time little Johnny will come running in with tear-streaked face complaining of the pain in his grazed knee. A quick hug, attention to the knee and a 'Oh look, isn't that Daddy home from work?' and the knee is forgotten as Johnny clambers onto the chair by the window to look for his father. Keep that sort of diversionary tactic up for several minutes and the pain of the knee will soon be forgotten.

This may be all very well for psyching yourself up for a visit to the dentist or for some pain that you are aware is coming your way, we can hear you say, but how do you deal with unexpected pain? How do you overcome the excruciating pain of having a steel girder fall on your foot or a pan of scalding water over your arm?

The answer simply is to deal with it in exactly the same way. This may be easier said than done, but if you want to cope with the pain then it *is* the most successful way. Screaming, shouting and dancing around uttering blasphemous obscenities are not useful ways of dealing with the situation. All you are doing then is rapidly raising your stress level and making it much harder for your pain defence mechanisms to cope. As in projected pain, the secret is to relax physically in order to enable the mind to relax as well. The more relaxed your body and mind are, the better you can cope with the pain. Self-punishing thoughts like 'How could I be so stupid as to leave that pan there?' or 'Why was I so silly as to think I could lift that beam on my own?' are negative responses which will only help fuel the pain. The immediate task is to start feeling good about yourself, use the techniques to block the pain, and thus diminish the hurt.

Chronic pain, such as that experienced after an operation, during rehabilitation or treatment for a wide range of ailments, or as a result of a particular disease (such as arthritis), requires a combination of the various procedures outlined in this book: an understanding of the background motivations and decisions that have led to the disease, creative visualisation, affirmation and blocking.

This is, very clearly, a way in which your thoughts and attitudes can influence the state of your body, its pain levels and the nerve messages you receive from it.

C H A P T E R    12
# THE FORCES OF HEALTH

It is one of the strange and regrettable things about the society in which we live that it is considered perfectly all right to be physically sick and see a doctor, but suffer emotionally or mentally and visit a psychiatrist and you are immediately labelled as some sort of nut case! In other words, it's okay to have physical needs and to risk expressing them. If they are not met the person to whom you have expressed them is considered to be at fault or inconsiderate. If, however, you express emotional needs and fears, you are often told to 'pull yourself together'. The net result may be that you end up more (emotionally) hurt than you were at the beginning and the other person is considered understanding and helpful!

It is interesting that in Eastern countries there is a much more relaxed attitude towards emotional and mental trauma. In Bali, for example, one common form of mental disorder is thought to be caused by evil spirits. The sufferer is treated by the local shaman or balian either by inducing trance-like states in the sufferer or perhaps the inhalation of certain herbal concoctions. Very often the balian's methods are successful and a cure is quickly achieved. This suggests that many cases of so-called mental illness are associated more with problems of day-to-day living rather than mental derangement.

In Bali, visiting a balian carries little of the stigma that visiting a psychiatrist does in the West, a stigma which is likely to reinforce the illness further. Furthermore, in Bali since blame is attached to the spirits rather than the patient, any stigma that might exist is lessened even further. The balian's role can perhaps be seen as a combination of priest, doctor and social worker, a function sadly lacking in Western society where the mental health professions have become increasingly medicalised and therefore carry the stigma of 'sickness' into the psychiatrist's consulting rooms.

This is not to say, of course, that there is no place for psychiatry in our world. But it is obvious that when dealing with the question of psychotherapy, whether it be from the point of view of the native witchdoctor or the Macquarie Street shrink, two factors are of paramount importance — the personal charisma of the therapist involved and the faith of the patient. Since the workings of the brain still remain largely a mystery to us, it is dangerous to drive a wedge between the faith-healer and the psychiatrist. The merits of their treatment should be judged by its effectiveness rather than the label put upon it.

It is a constant source of amazement that one of the most important skills we require in this life is not taught at schools — the skill of simply 'living'. From a very early age we all have to deal with our emotions, yet nowhere along the line are we ever given any guidelines about what to do. We are all given, as our very first present, the most intricate piece of machinery known to humankind, the brain. Yet we are left largely on our own to find out just how it works and how to get the best from it by a process of trial and error. It is scarcely surprising therefore that from time to time we find the whole thing overwhelming! The human brain, for all our deficiencies and inexperience, continues to think for us. The subconscious part continues to see us through the sticky times and work out, in quite incomprehensible ways, puzzles which we could sit over for years consciously trying to solve. If we let it, the brain could quite easily work without any input from us at all, but our lives would not necessarily be quite as we would like them!

Remember that through every human body there flows a basic lifeforce. It is called different names in different parts of the world: soul, Prana, Chi, lifeforce, etheric energy. Call it what you will, it is the positive force of growth and development and we all have it. As you may have realised by now this force is strongly influenced by the force of your thoughts. It is affected by your conscious thoughts which, in turn, affect your subconscious thoughts and the subconscious then feeds back what it thinks the conscious asked for, as in the following examples:

'Oh dear, I'm caught in the rain. I'm bound to catch a cold.'

'Mary's down with the flu again, I suppose everyone in the office will catch it now!'

'It's hayfever season again, I'll start sneezing any day now.'

And what does the poor old subconscious do? Fulfil your worst expectations like the good little thing it is!

It really is a case of 'Physician, heal thyself!' We have to realise that ultimately we alone are responsible for our well-being and we alone hold the power to heal ourselves.

Let's take a closer look at this business of healing and the life force that is within all of us. But first we'll do a small visualisation. Close your eyes and imagine if you will a world in which there were no healers — no doctors, no nurses, no hospitals, no naturopaths, no chiropractors, no natural health clinics. What would it be like? What would you do? How would you change your life to accommodate this state of affairs? Just ponder on that for a moment before we continue.

Is the whole thing too terrible to contemplate? Not really. After all, what happens if you cut yourself? Within a short time new skin tissue grows back and heals the wound. And what happens if you break an arm? In much the same way new bone growth occurs. In short, left to its own devices the body is capable of generating its own growth and maintenance, and keeping itself pretty healthy.

Nevertheless, we have developed a whole range of so-called healing methods over the ages to help these natural processes. Some are as natural as the body itself, others are much more intrusive. When it comes to the body, humans are rather like a small child with a new bike. It isn't long before the child is stripping it down, taking it to pieces and trying to put it back together again, with varying degrees of success. The lucky thing about all this is that the body is a most resilient piece of machinery and can put up with an enormous amount of tinkering before it starts to protest.

Here are just some of the different schools of healing that have developed in the world:

*Acupuncture* — a system of treatment using very fine steel needles inserted into specific points in the body in order to stimulate the body's internal healing mechanism.

*Alexander technique* — a way of releasing chronically-held tension patterns in order to facilitate natural reflexes of posture, balance and movement.

*Allopathy* — conventional drug medicine. A method of attacking illnesses with drugs and substances foreign to the body that are intended to stop the symptoms but can produce adverse side effects.

*Aroma therapy* — treatment using the aroma of herbs and other plants to balance body and emotional energies.

*Bach flower therapy* — treatment to balance the emotions through the use of specific flower extracts collected and treated in the way researched and developed by Dr E. Bach.

*Bioenergetics* — a treatment involving the release of pent-up emotions and re-uniting thinking and feeling processes through understanding the body's movement, energy and language.

*Body work* — deep tissue massage for muscular relaxation and emotional release.

*Chiropractic* — a healing system based on the theory that disease is caused by interference with nerve function and requiring readjustment of the spinal column.

*Faith-healing* — treatment of disease and illness by prayer and religious faith (*not* the debunked 'faith healing' of Asia).

*Fasting* — treatment by abstaining from all foods.

*Feldenkrais* — a treatment based on the teachings of Dr Moshe Feldenkrais who advocated the gentle and pleasant treatment of total posture without repetitive exercises.

*Gestalt* — a form of treatment which encourages the person to find the key to their own happiness and to rid themselves of old rigid patterns through self-awareness and experience. Role-playing, art, dance and dreams are all used in this therapy.

*Herbalism* — treatment with the use of medicinal herbs.

*Homoeopathy* — a way of treating disease with substances, given in minute potentised doses, which produce in a healthy person symptoms similar to those of the disease itself and give immunity.

*Hydropathy* — treatment of the body by the use of water.

*Iridology* — a method of diagnosis of the body's state of health by viewing the iris of the eye.

*Naturopathy* — a way of treating disease and disorders based on the use of natural substances, such as herbs, natural foods, exercise and sunlight.

*Neuro linguistic programming* — a system of coding behaviour. It applies the five senses of touch-feel, smell-taste, sight-vision, hear-listen and how people use language.

*Nutrition* — correcting health problems by manipulation of diet and the selective use of nutrients.

*Osteopathy* — a healing system based on the theory that disease is due to a deformation of some part of the body and can be cured by adjustment of that part.

*Physiotherapy* — a treatment of disease or bodily defects by physical activities such as massage, manipulations, gymnastics, etc.

*Psychiatry* — the science of treating mental illness through a combination of subconscious exploration and drug control.

*Psychodrama* — a type of group therapy in which the patients act out a theme of their own choosing which gives them an opportunity to express and resolve their own personal conflicts.

*Psychotherapy* — a form of treatment by way of an in-depth analysis looking for the 'unconscious processes' that motivate behaviour. No drugs are used.

*Rebirthing* — a system of conscious connected breathing that helps the individual to enter deep unconscious levels for examination and resolution of the physical, emotional and spiritual states.

*Reflexology* — a form of diagnosis and treatment focusing on the reflex points in the feet. Illness, poor nutrition and insufficient exercise reduces circulation in the feet causing crystalline deposits to form on the nerve endings. By applying deep pressure, these deposits are crushed and vitality is restored.

*Reiki healing* — treatment by the laying on of hands to channel universal life energy through the body in order to heal body, mind and spirit.

*Rolfing* — a method of very deep massage in which the practitioner manipulates the body in order to return it to a normal structural or postural position.

*Shamanism* — treatment brought about by invoking the spirit world.

*Shiatsu* — a physical therapy based on traditional Japanese techniques of diagnosis and treatment. It is a method in which the thumbs and palms of the hand are used to apply pressure to certain points of the physical body in order to correct irregularities.

*Somatic therapy* — an approach to stress developed by Wilhelm Reich and refined by Gerda Boyesen. It seeks to restore the body's natural stress regulatory system by bringing to the awareness events in early life which have limited one's enjoyment in the expression of life.

These are just some of the many different methods of healing that humankind has inventively come up with over the centuries. There are many more which you can add for yourself. One thing is immediately obvious however from this list. The treatments differ widely. Faced with the same disease a North American Indian medicine man is likely to take a completely different approach to that of a Macquarie Street specialist. It is quite possible, however, that they may have equal success when it comes to curing that disease.

At least some of the success of any treatment lies not in the skill of the practitioner, but rather in the belief of the patient that he is going to get better. This was understood by the very earliest healers who generally believed that sick people were in fact possessed by evil spirits, and once those spirits were driven out the person would get well again. If you now change 'evil spirits' to 'detructive or negative thoughts', you can see we have nearly come full circle. The witchdoctors of Africa, the medicine men of the American Indians and the balians of Indonesia all worked on this premise with equal success — and many still do! These were some of the earliest means of healing known. Eventually, as time progressed, some of these healers became more scientific and ended up as medical doctors. Others, concentrating more on the mind than the body, ended up as religious leaders.

Throughout time there have been literally thousands of recorded cases of people being healed through the power of the mind. The bible records in the Old Testament that an Israelite was healed of a snake bite simply by gazing at the snake. Could this be the first recorded case of mental homoeopathy? In the New Testament Jesus on several occasions uttered such words as 'Arise and walk, thy faith has made thee whole', and many seemingly miraculous cures were effected. Miraculous or not, true or not, the point here is that people found sufficient faith within *themselves* to heal their own bodies.

Even today thousands of people make their way annually to such shrines as Lourdes in France in the hopes of being cured of some disease or other. Some come away as afflicted as when they went. Others experience the 'miracle' of being healed. As we have seen, for this to be totally effective the subconscious has also got to believe that it will work.

Let us go back for a minute to the various forms of healing that we listed above. If they differ so widely, yet cures are still effected by them, then surely there must be some common underlying factor. Either there is a universal healing force which we activate with whatever healing technique we choose, or else there is a subtle passive force trying to keep our bodies in order and we distort this when we make ourselves ill. These different healing techniques merely remove the obstacles to this force and permit the body to heal itself.

We've already looked at the question of universal thought or intelligence, the great cosmic unconsciousness. If we can tap into this with our own subconscious, our own thoughts, then we must be able to stay well, or make ourselves ill and then make ourselves well again. It's an exciting thought, isn't it? The choice is yours.

# PHYSICIAN HEAL THYSELF!

In the middle of the eighteenth century, in the days before there were such useful inventions as refrigerators and deep freezers, one of the great problems in life was trying to keep the maggots out of the food. If you left the weekend joint lying around for too long, these nasty little white crawly things would appear. Despite endless jokes about the extra protein that they might provide, nobody liked them. Worse than that, nobody could explain where the hell they came from. The general assumption at the time was that they came about by spontaneous generation — that's to say they just happened.

Then in 1765 in Padua in Northern Italy an Italian naturalist by the name of Lazaro Spallanzani discovered that if you kept food in an airtight container the maggots didn't appear. In other words he discovered that there was no such thing as 'spontaneous generation' as everyone had believed, but rather that the maggots developed from invisible airborne larvae.

So much for spontaneous generation. Now in the twentieth century we have a phenomenon known as 'spontaneous remission'. This term is used to explain why people who are diagnosed as suffering from supposedly life-threatening diseases, such as cancer, suddenly appear to recover completely without any outside intervention. Nobody has ever quite understood how this occurs and the medical profession just shake their heads. Some doctors may even claim that their original diagnosis was wrong!

The truth of the matter is that the cure *has* been brought about by some sort of intervention, but we just don't know what it is. Could this be because we aren't looking in the right place for the answers, which has been the case so often in the past? Could it be that the answer in this instance lies not in medical intervention or physical intervention of any kind, but in the intervention of a positive mental attitude strong enough to turn the tide of the disease and create a healthy environment in the body in which the disease can no longer flourish?

The refusal of many members of the medical profession to believe that spontaneous remission is brought about by the power of the patient's mind is curious, considering their age-long belief in placebos. Since time immemorial patients have been given sugar-coated pills and 'lolly' water by their doctors, and have been cured of their supposed diseases in the mistaken belief that they have been fed genuine medicine. The placebo (from the Latin 'I shall please') is an invention of the medical profession and, in many ways, an indictment of it. That placebos should work at all is testimony to the deep-seated faith that doctors have instilled in people through the ages, a faith that is underpinned by the belief that only a doctor can make you better if you are ill. It is no surprise that in the old days the two most important people in any town were the priest and the doctor. It was to these two that people would turn, rather than the mayor or the sheriff. The doctor and the priest, the priest and the doctor, often interchangeable, frequently one and the same person. From the days of the early Greeks and Romans the doctor has been considered something of a demi-god, to be worshipped by society for his skill and understanding. Even today many Western societies still regard the doctor with near veneration, and his standing in the community ranks only a short way beneath royalty and the Church.

Because of his important position in the community the doctor was, and is, able to command a high price for his services. It is a near perfect set of conditions. Highly paid and on everyone's dinner party list, it is little wonder that the medical profession guard their position rigorously against all comers. If the community at large were ever to think that the doctor was little more than an ordinary mortal with only an average chance of either diagnosing your ailment or curing you, then his social standing, and subsequently his take-home pay, would surely come down. So too would his cure rate because your faith in him would naturally decrease. It is in a doctor's interests, therefore, to ensure that nothing topples him from his pedestal. This is not unlike the attitude that most orthodox Churches take towards religion.

The first thing that many doctors are liable to do when faced with a set of medical circumstances they do not understand is to ignore them and treat the immediately visible symptoms. To declare to the patient that he is quite stumped by the whole thing would inevitably lead to a severe loss of face and a consequent loss of confidence. Allow this to happen too often and people would sooner or later begin to realise that doctors are really only ordinary human beings who have spent seven years at medical school and have some, but by no means all, the answers. People would realise that perhaps the doctor's position in their esteem and in society should be no higher than that of a skilled accountant.

However we digress. The point is that the placebo,

which doctors have been happily doling out to some of their patients for years and years, works. It stands as proof that if the mind believes something to be so, then it is. If the mind believes that this sugar-coated pill is in fact a substance that will cure the disease, then cure it it frequently will. The effect is so powerful that we now have the 'double-blind placebo controlled' trials of new medicines. They are designed to eliminate the placebo effect from the results of the tests of new drugs.

One of the most dramatic stories about the startling effects of placebos concerns an American doctor by the name of Dr Bruno Klopfer. Klopfer was one of the researchers involved in testing a drug called Krebiozen which supposedly cured cancer. In 1950 the press was alive with stories about how effective the drug was in curing the disease and it attracted the attention of the American Medical Association. At this time Dr Klopfer had a patient who was critically ill, suffering from an advanced form of cancer throughout his body. When he discovered that Klopfer was involved in testing the new drug he asked to be treated with it. Within weeks he began to make an amazing recovery. In no time at all his tumours had started to disappear and he began to resume a normal life. Then the AMA's report on Krebiozen was published, stating that the drug was largely worthless. Almost immediately the patient's health began rapidly to deteriorate. Believing that desperate events called for desperate measures, Dr Klopfer told his patient that he now had an improved version of Krebiozen which would cure him, and Klopfer started to inject him with sterile water. Once again the patient began to make a dramatic recovery in the belief that the wonder drug could cure his cancer. Some time later the press again ran stories about Krebiozen, giving the results of exhaustive tests that had been carried out on it. They stated unequivocally that Krebiozen was useless in the cure of cancer. In less than three days Dr Klopfer's patient was dead! So there you have it, another example of the mind influencing the body. Even drugs work better when both the doctor and patient feel positive about them.

The placebo, it has been said, derives its power from the infinite capacity of the human mind for self-deception. In fact what it does is to transfer the mind's will to live into a physical reality. Since they have been shown to work, the evidence leads us to believe that there is no real separation between the body and the mind, and that illness of any kind is an interaction between the two.

Does this mean then that placebos make a nonsense of medical care? No, it doesn't, and despite the way it may sound to some this chapter is not intended to take a gratuitous knock at the medical profession. All we are saying is that the answer to the cure of any disease lies not in the hands of the doctor alone and the drugs he prescribes, but rather in the hands of the doctor *and* his patient. The placebo provides a means whereby the patient is able to think and believe that he will get well, and so start to cure himself and show the extent of his will to live. The placebo is, if you like, the catalyst and, properly used, is a powerful tool for good.

Of course, for every yin there is a yang. Placebos can have negative effects as well. Take, for example, the bone pointing ceremonies of the Australian Aborigines. If a tribe wishes to do away with one of its members for some reason, they mount an elaborate ceremony involving chanting and dancing. Then one of their number is deputed to take the bone and seek out the victim, who by this time is well aware of what is going on and has fled as far away as he can. Being the superb trackers that they are, it usually doesn't take long for the victim to be caught. The bone is then pointed at him, just that and no more. No hand is laid on him and no physical contact made. Usually within a month or so the victim is dead. He dies because he firmly believes he has no alternative. So powerful is his belief in the Aboriginal custom that no arguments of modern science will convince him that he can survive. The result is that his physical body functions begin to shut down and he dies.

To some extent we can see similar effects in Western societies when a patient is told by his doctor that he only has a short time to live. While he may exist from day-to-day as long as he is unaware just how sick he is, once told that he has only a given amount of time he will respond by not disappointing the doctor. If two months is all the time he's supposed to have left, then he will die in two months. It's the West's answer to Aboriginal bone pointing!

At this point let's return to spontaneous remissions. Told that he has only months to live, a patient can take quite a different tack. He can say to himself 'Like hell I have, I'll show them!' and live for month after month, kept alive by his determination not to die. If that determination is strong enough, the chances are that in time the patient may heal himself and again the doctors will shake their heads and say 'Perhaps our diagnosis was wrong in the first place'.

Your determination to live will enable you to heal yourself. The belief that you can survive against all odds, if you want to enough, is the medicine that you need to succeed. So perhaps the best medicine of all is to stop taking medicine and start exercising the mind.

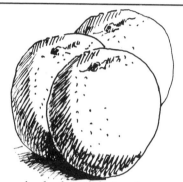

CHAPTER 14

# REBIRTHING — GOING BACKWARDS TO GO FORWARDS

In Chapter 4 we looked at life in the womb and its implications for personality formation. Let's return for a minute to that part of your development and consider a relatively new way of looking inside yourself, particularly at those crucial early times before, during and after birth when your personality was being shaped.

At the turn of the century Otto Rank, an Austrian psychoanalyst and a colleague of Sigmund Freud, argued that being born is a deeply disturbing experience, out of which all fundamental human conflicts stem. He said that everyone suffers from a secret wish to get back to the blissful state of the womb but at the same time feared to go there because of its association with the trauma associated with birth, particularly with traditional hospital births. Birth was our first close-up experience with death (death of the placenta, a part of our own body), plus pain and discomfort, and generally speaking it was not a happy time for most of us.

This theory did not gain much currency in the psycho-analytical world whose members tended to believe that since the child's personality wasn't formed until well after birth, these early happenings had no effect. As we have seen, this is untrue.

We now skip to the early 1970s and an American called Leonard Orr. Orr can rightly be dubbed the Archimedes of the twentieth century for, like his Greek forebear, it was in the bath that he made a major discovery which has the potential to change the lives of millions of people. One day, Orr was lying in a hot bath breathing deeply when he suddenly and unexpectedly experienced a great release of tension and a deep calmness. At first he thought that it must have been the hot water which had produced this wonderful effect on him, but some months later, after trying to recreate the event, he discovered that it was in fact the way he breathed.[1]

Orr had unconsciously been filling his lungs to the bottom with oxygen, letting it out and drawing in another breath without breaking the cycle. He called it 'Conscious Connected Breathing'. Oxygen, as we all know, is essential to the human body. Most of us use only the top third of our lungs when we breathe, and very often we forget to breathe at all! Holding one's breath is a common, though unconscious, pastime, particularly in moments of stress or fear.

What Orr was doing was consciously ensuring that every time he breathed he filled his lungs completely and allowed oxygen to circulate through his body in quantities far greater than usual. Many people at first confuse this with hyperventilation. In fact the two styles of breathing are quite different. While there may be an element of hysteria in hyperventilation, rebirthing breathing involves deeper and more relaxed connected breathing, and is only 'hyper' in the sense that it uses more air than usual.

Hyperventilation can, in fact, be beneficial to the body, even though it may produce some dramatic physical and emotional effects.[2]

It was these effects that Orr first experienced in his bath and which laid the foundations to the science of rebirthing. Why rebirthing? Well, many practitioners agree that it is perhaps an unfortunate appellation because of its quasi-religious connotations, but so far nobody has been able to come up with a better name. Orr called it rebirthing because, after practising it for some time, he actually experienced again the moment of his own birth. In so doing he made some startling revelations about his character and personality.

Before explaining in greater detail what rebirthing can do for you, let's just look at the technicalities for a moment. The process does not have to be done in the bath for a start! Since Orr discovered that it was the technique of breathing and not the venue that was the cause of his well-being, it became possible to rebirth lying comfortably on a mattress on the floor. The feeling of well-being is enhanced by being covered with a blanket which not only keeps you warm but offers you a feeling of security. This is known as a 'dry' rebirth and is the recommended starting point for all new rebirthees.

Once the rebirthee is settled, breathing can commence. It should continue for between forty-five and sixty minutes, and is done by breathing in and out, either through the nose or the mouth, but preferably the mouth, without stopping. This produces a greater flow of oxygen to the brain and to your system as a whole, which in turn generates a far higher level of energy in the body than we are used to. Appropriate soothing music can be played in the background to further create an atmosphere of calm and safety. At least to begin with you should be attended by a qualified rebirther who will help you through the process and provide you with further security so that you do not feel alone, abandoned or afraid.

Somatic psychotherapists believe that not all memory is necessarily stored in the brain, but that long-term memory is stored and distributed throughout all the cells of the body. By introducing large amounts of oxygen to them these cells are activated and the memory released. We often have 'blocks' in our cellular memory, such as traumatic events which we do not care to remember on a day-to-day basis. Imagine for example that you are sitting quietly reading this book when someone you know and love suddenly reaches across and hits you hard over the head with a bottle. The result, apart from the immediate physical pain and damage, is likely to be an on-going emotional trauma as well. For the next year or so you will probably jump back, as a purely protective reflex, when anyone suddenly reaches across you. But gradually the memory of that terrifying day will fade because you simply cannot carry it around in the forefront of your mind forever. Some people do carry traumas like this around which, because they are incapable for one reason or another of sublimating them, can drive them mad. Most people however will gradually allow the trauma to sink into their sub-conscious where it will be stored in the cellular memory.

This is rather like a wine cellar. Stored there are some really fine bottles of wine which have lain forgotten for years. But alongside them are some absolute stinkers which should have been decanted and drunk long ago and which by now have gone over the hill. Included in the emotional stinkers are all the traumas which you have experienced in your lifetime, starting with birth itself. There are now quite a few people who claim to have experienced going back into the womb during a rebirthing session and releasing this trauma. After birth there may have been the trauma of being separated from your mother and being taken off to a strange and noisy hospital nursery. There may have been the trauma of hearing the disappointed voice of your father saying he would have preferred a boy or a girl. Then again it may be something from a little later in life. One woman whom we have rebirthed remembered her parents playing a trick on her when she was about five years old. She heard a loud bang in the kitchen and called out to her parents to ask what it was. Her father told her not to worry, it was only Mummy exploding. Terrified, she ran into the kitchen to find her mother's shoes on the kitchen table and her mother nowhere in sight. Her mother had in fact hidden in the broom cupboard and did not come out for quite some time, leaving the child firmly convinced that Mummy *had* exploded and been fed through the mincer by her father. As you might imagine this pantomime, which had the parents in fits of laughter later, left a scar on the impressionable child which she carried with her to adulthood. She made various subconscious decisions at that time, among them that she could not trust her parents, or adults in general.

These and many others are the kinds of emotional blocks which we all carry around inside us. Rebirthing can expose all the influences and conditioning that you were unable to recall while making your lists earlier in this book. As we mentioned then, most of the time we have no idea they are there, but they are still working away in our subconscious, determining how we will act on different occasions and how we will relate to people and events. What we are attempting to do with rebirthing is to unlock these cellular memories, bring them out into the daylight (when you might, for example, use affirmation techniques), recognise them for what they are and make decisions about them based on our present knowledge of ourselves and the world in which we live.

It must be said here that rebirthing doesn't only awaken

'stinkers'. Many beautiful but long forgotten memories can also be awakened and enjoyed like drinking those fine wines which have been resting in the cellar all these years. Consequently you never really know what is going to happen during a rebirthing session. One day you can be laughing your head off and having the time of your life as you relive old happy memories, while the very next day you can be crying like a baby, recalling some unhappy event which you had long forgotten. Either way you are likely to come out of the session feeling lighter and happier, and released from some of the adverse effects of your past. It is unwise to go into a rebirthing session with any particular expectations. Few of them ever come about.

You might be lying there, breathing away, when suddenly you begin to experience pain in a part of your body, maybe your hands, your feet or your jaw. The feeling may be a tingling followed by a tightening of the muscles and some pain. This is called tetany and is fairly common in rebirthing. It is nothing to be frightened of, rather it is a sign that you have come across an emotional block through which energy will not pass. Now the breathing becomes all important. At this stage it must be maintained strongly, because it is the oxygen which will unlock that block and when it does the pain will go away. When the breakthrough takes place, you may need to yell or cry, but after the block is released you will feel a deep sense of relief usually followed by a relaxed period of calm.

You may not always know what it is that you have released, which can be very frustrating for some people. You will be aware that you have come up against an emotional block, you will breathe through it and feel it go away, but you may have to wait for weeks or months before you realise what it is you have given away. One day it will dawn on you suddenly that something in your life is missing. Either your temper has improved or you have lost your irrational fear of heights or the desire to smoke. It could be any one of a thousand different things.

It is important to remember that the brain, being the wonderful organ that it is, will not allow you to hurt yourself. This is clearly shown in cases of hypnosis where the hypnotist can easily get you to stand on a chair and pretend you are a chicken but however much he asks he cannot get you to jump out of a window. Consequently, if the brain decides that a particular trauma which you have buried away is too much to bear all in one go, it will not confront you with it directly during a rebirthing session. Instead the layers of the trauma will be peeled back in much the same way as you peel an onion. Slowly you will get closer and closer to the juicy bit at the centre, but it may take four, five or even ten or more rebirthing sessions before you see the full trauma. By this time you are well aware that there is something there to be examined and that the brain is holding you back. You are, in short, being softened up for the experience and when it eventually comes it is with such a feeling of relief that you do not feel nearly so bad about it. By this time too you are better equipped to deal with whatever it is.

Of course there are those people who do not necessarily have any emotional blocks they wish to deal with. Rebirthing works just as well for them but on another plane. By supplying the brain with greater than usual amounts of oxygen the rebirthee will stimulate the right hemisphere particularly, causing a much higher level of awareness. This can include such effects as seeing brighter colours, vivid images or all the other experiences usually associated with taking psychedelic drugs. The great beauty of this process, unlike magic mushrooms, LSD, marijuana and so on, is that oxygen is absolutely free and absolutely legal!

Another great beauty of rebirthing is that after you have had about ten sessions accompanied by an experienced rebirther you can continue the process on your own. It is just about the only way of getting in touch with your subconscious and working out your problems that can be done without having to pay large regular amounts of money to see a practitioner. Of course it is still a good idea to have a rebirther in attendance from time to time to help you if you come up against blocks that you cannot seem to clear on your own.

As well as 'dry' rebirthing, you can also re-create the experience of Leonard Orr and have 'wet' rebirths. One method is to rebirth in a tub heated to 40°C, the heat in which you floated in the womb, lying face down and breathing through a snorkel. The rebirther stands in the water supporting you around the hips and making sure that the top of the snorkel doesn't go under the water. This is a powerful process, particularly if you have emotional blocks surrounding your birth, as the recreation of a womb-like situation can release many memories.

The other method is a cold wet rebirth. The process involves slowly getting into the tub of cold water. You start the breathing outside the tub and begin by putting just one foot in. Keeping your breathing regular, you slowly immerse yourself a bit at a time. The rebirth is usually completed once you have managed to immerse your whole body in the tub. This is a completely different sort of rebirth. The cold water brings up basic urges such as the death urge, and the shivering and shaking that usually accompanies a cold rebirth are more to do with these urges than with the temperature of the water. This kind of rebirth can be a powerful experience, too.

Imagine the human body to be like a mainframe computer which needs a basic systems disc to run on. If there is a fault in the disc, then every time you push a particular key the fault will come up again and again. The only way to correct it is to go back into the system, find the fault and correct it. So it is with rebirthing. If you react in certain unfavourable ways to a set of circumstances it is probably because you have been programmed at birth or soon after to do so. If you wish to change that reaction, you must go back, find the moment in which it was formed, and change it for a more suitable one.

The purpose of rebirthing is to examine all those early programmes which have been fed into you and decide whether or not they are appropriate for your life today. It is no longer necessary to live with the hand that you thought you were dealt at birth. Rebirthing is a way of chucking in some of the cards and exchanging them for new ones.

# LOVE ME, LOVE MY ULCER

There are a number of illnesses which, on the face of it at least, appear to be inherited and, therefore, inevitable. Some of the ones which immediately spring to mind are cancer, heart disease, obesity, asthma and arthritis. But just how inevitable are these? Working on the belief that you can consciously or subconsciously create your own illness, it must be assumed, if you have one or more of these, that you gave them to yourself for some reason. And what more powerful reason than that your mother or father, grandmother or grandfather also had them?

Yes, that's right. You in fact create traditional, acceptable, hereditary diseases. If you don't believe it try this test. The next time someone tells you how bad their arthritis is, ask them if any other member of their family ever suffered from it. The chances are more than even that their reply will go something along these lines 'Oh, yes. My mother used to suffer terribly from it and her mother before her!' The result, of course, is that after spending years listening to mother and grandmother complaining about their arthritis you are expecting to get it too, and sure enough if that is your attitude the time will come when you do. Bingo! A self-fulfilling prophesy, which allows you to explain to anyone who will listen, 'You see, it runs in the family'.

There are, in fact, very few 'hereditary' diseases that you absolutely can't avoid. Many illnesses may 'run in families', yet it is possible for you to choose *not* to succumb to them if you are sufficiently determined to make the necessary changes to your diet, lifestyle and mental attitude. Consequently it would not matter that four generations of your family had died from heart attacks if you led a healthy lifestyle, ate well, exercised regularly and kept relatively free from stress. Under these conditions the chances of you becoming the fifth generation to die early in this way would be low. If, on the other hand, you were convinced you were going to succumb to heart failure at an early age and unthinkingly encouraged a lifestyle that would produce that result, then die from this cause you surely will. Indeed, even those difficult genetic diseases such as haemophilia which you may be born with, can, with enough faith and determination (and time), conceivably be conquered.

Many of the more common diseases are largely environmental in origin. In the Western world these include cardiovascular problems, arthritis, hypertension, obesity, asthma and cancer. In Third World countries they include a variety of infectious diseases. There are always ways around these illnesses: it is largely a matter of the way in which you perceive them and what you choose to do about them as to whether or not they become life-threatening for you or not. In treating any such condition, the physician should first look at the psychodynamics of the family as a whole. Believe it or not, there are actually diseases which are acceptable in a family and others which are not!

In some families, for example, only physical problems

are acceptable. You can break as many bones as you like and be looked on as something of a go-getter. In other families such physical disintegration is abhorred, while subtle frailties are deemed to be 'elegant', rather like those of Jane Austen heroines who were always swooning dead away with the vapours. Now that's a perfectly acceptable collapse in some households. Heart disease is also acceptable in some families. After all it can be a family tradition!

Family patterning plays an important part in our health, in combination with our genetic make-up: the two combine to produce the results. This manifests itself clearly when you get different people faced with the same stresses but reacting in quite different ways. For example, one person may succumb to the stress by getting a duodenal ulcer whilst another person, after being subjected to exactly the same stresses, will react by having a heart attack, a third may have no reaction at all or indeed may thrive on the situation. Here the genetic make-up plays a big part and how you are affected depends on which part of you is the weakest and most vulnerable. But frequently it is difficult, if not impossible, to separate the effects of family patterning and genetic make-up. Having said that, however, it is interesting to note that a recent study done among adopted children showed that 98 per cent of the children under review were prone to the same illnesses as the other members of their adopted family. So although genes undoubtedly play some part in the decision as to how you are going to react to particular stresses in your life, the traditional and acceptable reaction in your family will play a major role.

Childish emulation is another player in this health drama. We know of one case where a young girl was prone to the most painful migraines which usually resulted in her gaining a lot of sympathy from the members of her family. Determined not to be outdone, the younger sister tried desperately to give herself similar migraines and eventually succeeded! The migraines miraculously stopped when the elder sister left home and the younger girl inherited all the attention. Another example is the six-year-old boy who sees his father frequently cutting his finger and subconsciously encourages similar accidents so that he too can bleed like Daddy!

Your sex can also play a role in the type of illness you are 'allowed' to have. For example, it's considered acceptable for men to get angry, and when they consequently succumb to ulcers it's considered to be an acceptable male complaint. If you think about it, it's considered very odd for a woman to get an ulcer. If, on the other hand, you are a woman, then nobody thinks badly of you if you keep bursting into tears; depression is considered an acceptable illness for females. Men who suffer from depression are frequently considered to be somewhat suspect.

Then there are the cultural aspects of illness. Nowadays in Western countries illnesses like cancer and heart attacks are deemed 'acceptable'. The statistics for deaths related to these illnesses are so high that it has now become an accepted way of departing this life. In Third World countries, however, far fewer people die from heart attacks, which are a sign of 'out of place' Western affluence. Conversely sickness brought about by infection, for example cholera or similar diseases, is more likely to be contracted and to be acceptable. These diseases would be completely unacceptable in the antiseptic Western world where people equate them with a lack of hygiene. Likewise in the Third World, illness brought about by 'possession by evil spirits' (what we might call schizophrenia or other similar mental illnesses) is considered perfectly credible and is considerably less censured than mental illness is in Westernised societies.

Every one of us has our own understanding of the need for health and ill-health buried within us and often we will subconsciously express our decisions without realising it. For example, how often have you said something like 'I'd die if my son were to join the army', or again, 'I just couldn't stand it if my husband left me'. Those simple metaphors can speak volumes about your deep-seated beliefs. There have been numerous documented cases of people who, having expressed the belief jokingly that they would die if something or other happened in their lives, have been faced with the event and have actually become terminally ill. Many people who have said frequently that they couldn't stand the loss of their spouse, when faced with death or desertion, physically collapse and may even die themselves or go into a dangerous decline. What can you learn about yourself from your expressions? Think about some of the things you commonly say and see if there is a lesson to be learnt from them. What you say does not necessarily mean you are going to live up to your threat, but it does give an indication of your deep-seated fears and other emotions. Your subconscious speaks to you in strange ways.

It is important to realise that there is a strong and indelible link between your mind and your body. There is ample evidence to believe that we think, not only with our brains, but with our whole bodies. Our physical state is in fact a manifestation of our mental state. It can be said, therefore, that our bodies are an expression of our thoughts and that illness is distorted thought in a physical form.

If this is so, then by changing the thought you can change the physical form of your body. In other words, by changing the thought you can actually change your health. The cells in your body are forever reproducing at a rate of which even the rabbit world would be proud. Believe it or not the average human body creates one million new red blood cells every second, to say nothing of the thousands of other cells in our bodies which are being recreated at a rapid rate. Every second of our life new cells are being born and old ones are dying. Every seven years our entire body has undergone a complete cellular change. Think about it. If we accept that our thoughts can alter our physical state, then we have the power to influence these millions of new cells every time they are formed. Quite clearly we possess a powerful vehicle for change, be it for better or worse.

An amusing and illuminating experiment in this area was conducted some years ago at Stanford University in America by Dr A. L. Bloomfield. Dr Bloomfield placed a number of volunteers in an isolated room and asked them to talk about their favourite foods. Before entering the room their gastric hydrochloric acid (HCl) was measured and further measurements were taken after their discussion. Following the conversation about food it was found that the volunteers' gastric HCl had risen by up to six-fold, proving that the mere thought of food was sufficient to produce a physical result in the stomach. What is more, these volunteers were given no specific direction to set about raising their gastric HCl. All they were thinking about was eating, which in turn produced the result of raising the gastric HCl. The point of this is that very often one particular action can trigger off quite a different effect and a thought can have an unexpected effect at a tangent to the original idea.

# SINGING THE BLUES

The life and times of famous American Blues singer, Billie Holliday, serves as a powerful example of how we often allow other people to adversely affect our lives, often to nobody's benefit. Too often these are people whom we love and respect, which makes it even worse.

Holliday first made her name in the 1930s with her deeply soulful rendition of the American negro Blues songs. Her influence was carried on by such later greats as Louis Armstrong and Charlie Parker. Her name was to become a legend. Sadly, like most legends, there was a large degree of unreality about her life which ended at the tragically early age of forty-four. It is the cause of her death in which we are interested.

Holliday and her ambitious manager had been on the road for several months, giving sell-out concerts over the length and breadth of America. Billie was exhausted and longed to get back to her husband and children so that she could rest. One night, almost crippled by exhaustion, she suddenly cancelled her appearance and announced that she was going home. Her manager was appalled. After a long and bitter scene in her hotel room, he convinced her that such an action would certainly ruin her career. He persuaded her to keep going and finish the tour as planned. Reluctantly Billie agreed, but as she became more and more tired she turned to drugs to keep her going. Pills and alcohol were the only things that could see her through each day, and from that moment on, her life started going downhill. The tour ended, but by that time she was hooked and she died not long afterwards.

It is all too easy to sacrifice your life for others, for those you love and trust, or for those to whom you feel you owe a duty. Sadly, all too often no-one benefits in the long run. For example, John and Susan's mother had remained single after her divorce, saying that she had to take care of the children and, for their sakes, couldn't have a social life of her own. But she became bitter and depressed and often found herself taking it out on the children. Several years later Susan told us that she used to wish her mother had remarried so that they could have been a big happy family again. She felt guilty about her mother's loneliness.

Many seeming setbacks turn out to be opportunities. Xandria used to play competition tennis, until one day she had a car crash (not her fault on the surface of it!) and as a result she was no longer able to serve the ball effectively. From then on serious tennis was out. At first she railed against a fate that had totally altered her previously busy and social weekends centred round the tennis court. Then she thought, 'Let's assume I *did* create this for myself. What do I stand to gain from it?' She quickly discovered that there were a lot of other things she wanted to do at weekends, including putting together the Choosing Health Intentionally seminar, which would probably have remained undone to this day had the accident not given her the time.

Michael used to ride horses, trained a showjumper and had aspired to become a polo player. Following a couple of nasty falls he developed a bad back which forced him to give up the sport. Looking back, he now realises that the reason he developed the bad back and allowed it to flourish was because he was aware that he wasn't a very good rider and was, in fact, not a little frightened of what he did half the time! The bad back was an excellent face-saver at the time but became a dreadful nuisance later on. Such ailments can, of course, be cured through a process of self awareness, acknowledgment of motivation and a firm desire to bring about renewed health — but it does take time.

So we all, in one way or another, tend to limit ourselves as we go through life. You probably have as well. Just sit quietly for a minute and think of the times in your life when you have felt powerless, when you have wanted to change your life but have felt unable to do so. Write down your thoughts. Now think of the times when you let an outside event stop you doing something you wanted to do or prevent you having something you really wanted. Write them down as well. Consider what you have lost and what it may have cost you, and write that down, too. Now ask yourself the following questions:

Who or what stopped me having what I wanted?
Who or what stopped me being what I wanted to be?
Who made me accept a substitute?
Who did I give my power away to?
What was the long-term outcome of this?
Did they win?
Did I benefit?
What was my real fear?

When you have written down the answers to these questions, think about them carefully for a minute. Now go back to one of the original situations and try to imagine what would have happened if you had followed your own aims rather than allowing someone else to divert you. Use the full rein of your imagination to create the best possible outcome for everyone involved. What would have happened to you? What would have happened to the other people involved? Now write *those* thoughts down.

What you should have by now is a complete scenario of, firstly, how you allowed yourself to be sidetracked by other people and, secondly, what the outcome might have been if you had decided to follow your own devices. Which is the better scenario of the two? Is it not often the case that you have sacrified yourself for some perceived benefit to someone else, and later discovered that it would have been a whole heap better for all concerned if you had followed your own needs from the start? Just remember the story of Billie Holliday the next time you are thinking of giving away your power to someone else and work out if it might not be better to stick to your own intuition. Recognise, too, that you *are* probably doing exactly what you want, merely using the other person as an excuse to rationalise your actions and decisions.

Very often we don't allow ourselves enough time to really appreciate exactly what it is we do want out of life. We drift through it from day to day, often believing that we are happy, contented and doing the right thing, only to discover in middle age that life has suddenly become rather meaningless and that we have been on the wrong track. What glossy magazines and some psychiatrists call the 'mid-life crisis' is in fact no more than the sudden realisation that we have been wasting our time. We may have been allowing other people to dictate our lifestyles, or perhaps we have simply not stopped long enough to work out what we really want out of life. Those people who have a single-minded commitment to a cause and pursue it from cradle to grave don't suffer from this so-called crisis. They know what they want and how to get it. It's the rest of us who don't have the benefit of such a goal who fall prey to doubts and create a crisis of confidence around ourselves.

Bearing in mind the old maxim that today is the first day of the rest of your life, take a sheet of paper and write down now a list of all the things you would like to be doing with your life but are not. It can be absolutely anything that you want out of life. For example,

> I want to improve my education
> I want to give up smoking
> I want to learn to play bridge
> I want to get a better paid job
> I want a larger house

Now opposite that list write your reasons for not doing these things. For example, you might find,

> I want to improve my education *but* I don't have enough time to go to night school
> I want to give up smoking *but* I am too weak-willed
> I want to learn to play bridge *but* nobody will play with me
> I want to get a better paid job *but* I am not qualified enough
> I want a larger house *but* I cannot afford it

Next write down what you would have to do or what would have to happen for you to accomplish these desires. Then ask yourself if you are prepared to do what is necessary to make your wish possible. If you are prepared to, then *do it*!

If you are not prepared to, then ask yourself why not.

It may be that there was a desire even greater than that which prevents you. For example, by not following your own wishes you may be saving your marriage or benefiting your children. If this is the case, then recognise the reasons why you have given up your desires. Realise that you gave up these desires voluntarily. By doing so you won't then have to make yourself ill to get even with yourself or someone else for your sacrifice.

Above all, make time for yourself so that you can examine your life day by day to discover if you are doing the things you really want to do. Make lists of your ambitions frequently and strive to achieve them. It helps to write down what you want, why you think you can or cannot achieve it, and what has to be done if you *are* to achieve it. Somehow it's not quite so easy to fool yourself when you see it written in black and white!

We have often found that a person can come to a whole new understanding of themselves within a very short space of time this way. The results are often surprising. If you try it with your own life there's a good chance that you won't be found singing the blues when you turn forty or fifty!

# HEALTH IS A RISKY BUSINESS

To become healthy you have to take risks. The first, and possibly biggest, risk is to take complete responsibility for your own health. If you are to be truly healthy then you cannot pass the buck to someone else. You have to acknowledge that the road to health is the one which has to be built by you, not by some outside contractor. This can be a little scary to begin with because you will have to break up the old road first. But, rather like a good horror movie, there's nothing like the odd scare to get the adrenalin going!

How serious are you now about wanting to do something to improve your health, both physically and emotionally? You are serious? Even so, watch those little evasive tactics which creep in to all our best intentions — waiting till the time feels right, or the children go back to school, or you're better organised. We all do it, so there's no need to feel guilty, just be aware of them.

Think of a time when you promised yourself that you would do something like losing weight, improving your diet, or giving up smoking or alcohol. Can you think of such a time? Now write down a list of all the reasons you gave yourself for not doing it immediately. You know the sort of thing, 'I'll start my diet tomorrow', or 'I'll give up drinking after Mark's wedding next month'. What you were really saying to yourself was 'I'm not ready to give it up yet', or 'I don't really want to', or even 'I don't see why I should but it is expected of me'. Well, that's fine, too, so long as you recognise it for what it is. Rather than giving yourself a hard time about not giving up, acknowledge that you simply are not ready to take action at this time and tell yourself that you will try again when you are ready.

The secret is to be aware of your true feelings. For example, the next time a situation arises and you change the subject, or walk away, or gaze out of the window or make a cup of tea, stop and ask yourself what is *really* happening. When you decide to end a relationship or to create a new one, when you procrastinate rather than get on with a job, or create an accident for yourself, stop and think about it. What is the core issue that has prompted the action or non-action? Things rarely happen for the reason you initially think.

It is important to get in touch with the subconscious reasons, if you can, for delaying any decision to get well. You will often suppress a problem by treating just the symptoms. You may take drugs or have an operation, change your diet or stuff yourself full of vitamins and minerals. Nevertheless, if you haven't come to terms with the root cause of the illness, you will find the need to sabotage the treatment or, worse still, create a further, possibly even more severe, illness later to take the place of the first one.

There's a relatively simple way of finding out how and why you are sabotaging your health. You need a piece of paper, a pencil and a willing friend. When you have all three, write a list of ten things to do with either your physical or emotional self starting 'I should. . . .'. For example, 'I should give up cigarettes' or 'I should take some exercise' or 'I should show my feelings to my spouse more'. Then one by one read them out to your friend. After each one the friend should simply ask, 'Why?' Answer them truthfully, or as truthfully as you can. Your friend then asks 'Why don't/haven't you?' Answer that question and from the answer see if you can work out between you what this tells you about yourself and your beliefs. Of course this process is only going to work if you tell the truth as you see it. Making up answers to justify your decision is like cheating at Patience.

Now home in on one major health problem which concerns you at this moment. It could be asthma, or rheumatism, or simply a feeling of continual tiredness. Complete the statement: 'The reason I have. . . is because . . .' Do this several times and write down the answers. Next complete the statement: 'The main reason I have. . . is because. . .' Then complete one further statement: 'A benefit I derive from having. . . is. . . .' Write down a list of the necessary or possible treatments for your condition and ask yourself if you wish to have that treatment. Put the answer clearly in writing and commit yourself to it by signing and dating the statement. This will serve as a useful reminder to you in the weeks and months ahead and you can keep referring back to this process for moral support when the going gets tough.

People who are unsuccessfully trying to give up an addiction or failing to improve their health are often accused of lack of moral fibre. This is not, as we have seen, the truth at all. It is not the moral fibre that is lacking, merely the will to succeed in the first place. Lack of will to succeed is the result of either not subconsciously acknowledging the presence of the addiction or not feeling that you are ready yet to let go of it without it being replaced by something equally injurious to you. Without this subconscious understanding your journey along the path of better health will be as arduous as toiling up the Himalaya with a thirty-kilo gas heater on your back.

The next thing is to recognise the role of programming in your childhood. Think back to the chapters on pre-birth and childhood influences, and conditioning, and remember what the lessons explained about the way you were programmed. Consider whether or not these belief patterns are serving your best interests now. Has the time come to let the past go? Forgive the past — and that usually means your parents! — for what may have happened. What is forgiveness? Think about it. It's simply a decision to stop beating yourself up.

Try doing that now. Close your eyes and picture your mother and father or whoever brought you up. Think of the things they have done or said to you that may make you feel angry with them. When did they do or say these things? Picture the details if you can. How did you feel at the time? What were you saying to yourself and what were you saying out loud? What were you wishing you could say at the time? What have you wished since, that you had said? Who else was there? How were you relating to them?

Now consider what it was really all about. What are you really angry about? What are you afraid of? Very often things that we cannot forgive others for are the things we cannot forgive ourselves for. Realise that as the master of your destiny you can in fact forgive and drop this issue whenever you are ready. It's up to you.

To clear up a situation that has made you angry, or to make it right with a person who has angered you, it is not necessary to confront that situation or person directly. The decision to be angry is entirely within yourself. If you wish to finish it, you must first ask yourself what would have to happen, or be said, for the matter to be cleared up. Then consider what advantages there may be, if any, in *not* clearing up the situation. Then look at the cost of not clearing it up. If you decide that there are no advantages or the cost of continuing the situation is too high, then make whatever statement is necessary to mend it. You can simply make the statement to yourself because, after all, the problem lies within you and only you have the power to alter it.

If the problem lies with your parents, and most of us can find something to blame our poor parents for, resolve to learn more about them. Ask them about *their* childhoods and try to find out the sort of programming they received from their parents. Remember that they too have been labouring under the burden of being human and are only as good as the programming they received. We are all victims of victims of victims. Understand, if you can, that they did their best for you according to the patterns of their own upbringing, so try to feel compassion for their lives. Doesn't it feel easier now for you to understand them and so forgive them and start loving them unconditionally? If you have children of your own you will probably find this easier to do.

Remember what has been said previously about children. They recognise from a very early age that 'big people' are essential to their survival and that they must be pleased for protection to be assured. These big people establish the norms in your life and are inherently right. It takes a great deal to destroy this love. Equally, once it is destroyed it can be very difficult to resurrect. If your love for your parents has been destroyed, and you can manage to rebuild it now, you will have achieved something really major in your life. If you can do that, you can do just about anything else you set your mind to. You can certainly create a healthy future for yourself exactly the way you want it to be.

When all is said and done the major relationship in life is with yourself. All other relationships will reflect this one back to you. Your relationships with your parents, with your children, with your spouse and your friends, are all reflections of the relationship you have with yourself. How easy is it to love someone else, or have them love you, when you do not love yourself? Not easy at all. It is a fact that you will tend to attract people who will treat you the same way as you treat yourself. For example, if you have continual self doubts and are very hard on yourself, you will inevitably attract people who will nurture that doubt and be hard on you. We are, in a sense, our own best friend and our own worst enemy at the same time.

Likewise, if you don't trust yourself, then inevitably you will attract people who won't trust you either. There is an old adage which says that you can judge a person by their friends. What this means is that you can see from the kind of friends a person has, and the relationship between them, what the person feels about themselves.

To make it easier to love yourself, first get in touch with the little child within you and learn to love him or her. One good way to do this is to get a photograph of yourself as a toddler and speak to it. This technique is not advised for use in public places, but can be very effective when done in the privacy of your own room. Recognise the child and give it messages of unconditional love and approval. Recreate this child as an imaginary companion and, from time to time, ask it what it wants to do. It is important that the little child in all of us also gets a chance to have some fun. You cannot go on being boringly grown-up all the time, occasionally you need to kick up your heels and give your little child an airing. This is a good thing. It is an acknowledgment of your existence, your life and what you are and have been. Throwing off your Dior gown or three-piece suit and diving into the nearest fountain without a thought for the local constabulary can, on one level, be considered an excellent thing to do. If everyone were able to get in touch with the small child within them frequently and take them out to play, the world would be a happier place and diving into fountains wouldn't be against the law!

Since other people are notoriously bad at taking care of you, you had best learn quickly how to take care of yourself; at the same time allow other people to take care of themselves. Then you can share your complete self with other complete selves. However, you don't have to take care of yourself entirely alone if you don't want to. You can enlist the help of others, but do so openly. Learn to ask for your needs to be met directly rather than indirectly. For example, if you want someone to spend time with you because you want the company, ask them to do just that. Don't offer a devious invitation like drinks or the movies and then get hurt if they say no. Not being direct leaves you open to interpreting their answer as a rejection of yourself, rather than just a rejection of the movie. Ask the question directly and honestly and you will get the evening you really want.

The other thing to remember when it comes to looking after yourself is that you must learn to love yourself as you are now. There is no future in telling yourself that you will love yourself when you are a better person. Acknowledge all the things that you are at this moment. Feel proud of all the things about you that are to your liking and calmly assess those things that could benefit from a change. Loving yourself just the way you are is the first and most important step to attaining good physical and emotional health. Before you draw back in horror and say

'How self-centered!', think for a moment. What is wrong with loving yourself? It needn't (and shouldn't) stop you wanting to change, to grow and to improve. And anyway why shouldn't you like yourself? After all, if you don't like yourself, why should anyone else? You know yourself better than anyone else ever can and if you broadcast to the world by subtle signs and deeds as well as by what you think and say, that you are not very likeable, then why wouldn't they believe you and start to feel the same way? It all comes from those childhood messages that you shouldn't 'push yourself forward', or 'boast about your achievements', or 'claim to be good at something'. By the time this was thoroughly drummed into you, you knew, or at least your subconscious did, that you were not as good as the next person.

Having said this, however, does not mean there is open slather on boastfulness or self-aggrandisement. It's simply a suggestion that you acknowledge, at least to yourself, your good points, and accept all the other ones so that you can get on with the business of becoming the person you want to be.

If you aren't too keen on yourself right at this moment or feel that you need bolstering up a bit, grab a mirror and look at your face closely. Then say to your image 'I love and accept you exactly as you are'. This exercise was developed by Louise Hay, American healer and author of *You Can Heal Your Life*, and, although you can be guaranteed to feel as foolish as a fish on a bicycle to begin with, you will soon get used to the exercise. The effects can be astonishing. It is well worth the initial embarrassment.

To get what you want out of life, you must focus on what does work for you, not what doesn't. Concentrate on your good points, not your bad ones, and concentrate on the desired outcome of your life rather than wasting time proving your own point or proving someone else wrong. If you don't like what someone else is doing, you don't have to put up with it. You have the power to change it. But you won't change it by attacking the other person, because they will only become angry, defensive and resentful. Instead state clearly that you like them, then, and only then, explain exactly how you feel, how that feeling results from what they are doing, and how you would like them to change. By being absolutely clear on your desired outcome, the results should be to your liking. Of course you can't win all the time, but if the other person refuses to acknowledge your feelings, then you will have to reassess your relationship with them.

This is it then. We are nearing the end of this journey to self-awareness and you should now consider setting yourself some goals to ensure your healthy future. Goals give you something to live for and aim for. They should cover your home and family life, any special relationships you may have, your finances, religion, work and career, fun, hobbies and recreation, and exercise, as well as your health, looks, weight, and so on. All goals should be specific, measurable, possible, designed for short- and long-term, and (just) realistic!

List your emotional, mental and physical goals and then imagine that you are a child again but with all your present wisdom. Ask yourself the question 'What do I want to be when I grow up?' Now write down a list of goals for everything that you want in the future. Writing them down is important because it will do a number of things. First, it will convince the subconscious that you expect to get better and will give a meaning to the effort you make. By directing your thoughts you are creating a positive reality, and by making this list you are affirming that you have the power to create your life as you want it. Second, will it help you to establish your priorities and to refocus if you are the sort of person who has always put other people's needs ahead of your own.

Once you have completed your list re-read it, then, taking one goal at a time, close your eyes and visualise yourself achieving that goal. Create a clear picture of it happening — how it feels, how it looks, how it sounds. Valerie M used this technique successfully. Having just turned fifty, she was bored with her marriage and irritated by her husband Ted. She immediately set down her goals: to be single, to have a good time, and to be free from all domestic chores. However once she had created this scenario for herself she suddenly found that a divorce would mean that she would be living alone and she would be lonely. Also, she realised that there would still be domestic chores to do, she would still have financial problems and that much of her social life, which she did enjoy, depended on her being one of a couple. When she thought about it further she realised that there were in fact a lot of benefits to the marriage, so she set about finding ways to improve it rather than trying to pull it to pieces.

Sort out any conclusions that you might draw as a result of achieving your goal. Then when the picture is completely clear, make a fist of one hand and thump it into the palm of the other, saying silently to yourself as you do it, 'Yes, this is what I want to have. This is what I want to do. This is what I want to be.'

Work through your whole list of goals in this way, affirming each one once the picture is clear in your mind, and know that this is exactly how your life will be in the future. Check your goals every day and concentrate on achieving them. Resolve to concentrate on emotions that are in harmony with the universe, such as love, generosity, trust, hope, faith, confidence and honesty, to help you achieve these goals. Resolve at the same time to forgo all discordant emotions such as hate, jealousy, selfishness, pity, despair, fear and deceit, for these will only sap away your will to succeed.

If anything happens in your life that you don't like, ask yourself, 'What did I do to cause or contribute to that?' Then go on to ask what it tells you about yourself, what can you learn from it, and what benefit can you derive from it? It is easy to blame other people and say 'I didn't cause that', but you should recognise your own power, because, in some way, you did cause it, even if only by being present at the time.

# CHANGING THE MONKEY ON YOUR BACK

One of the main reasons that we become unhappy and fearful, and eventually ill, is because there are some things which we convince ourselves we simply must have. For each of us these 'must haves' are different and you can probably think up a whole list of examples for yourself. Here are some of the more common ones:

If only I had more money...
If only I had a particular job...
If only I could own my own house...
If only I could have a loving partner...
If only I could stay at my ideal weight...
If only my family would leave me alone...
If only I looked more attractive...
If only my partner was faithful...
If only I had perfect health...

We convince ourselves that if we only had one or more of the things on our list then everything would be all right, everything would be perfect and we could transform the rest of our lives. But it doesn't work that way, does it? Why? For the simple reason that, while you don't have 'it' you are miserable but when you do have 'it' you are terrified of losing it. In fact, 'it' is those wants that we have in life which take on the proportions of an addiction rather than a mere need. You don't relax when you attain what you have been seeking because human nature compels you to keep seeking more and to worry endlessly about retaining what you have already acquired.

So that you can relax, you need to change the status of these 'must haves' from addictions to simple preferences. For example, if you are 'addicted' to your spouse, you are dependent on them and you will fall apart if they leave you. But you can't be happy with them because you are scared that they are going to leave you. So you can't be happy with them and you can't be happy without them. On the other hand, if you simply *prefer* to be with your spouse, then you can share with them freely, manage without them, love them freely, feel secure in your togetherness and not be jealous.

As long as you are addicted to something you cannot be free. This applies as much to social needs and other people as it does to the more common addictions such as drugs and alcohol. To be free you have to be able to do without the support of these addictions. That means taking complete responsibility for yourself and accepting the fact that you cannot rely on others to support you. It doesn't mean, however, that you have to be lonely. What is required is a downgrading of the addiction to a preference, or, in other words, a change of attitude.

Take a moment now to list all the things currently in your life which you could change if you wanted to. Then write a list of all those things which you *cannot* change. Now look for the common denominator in the list of things that you can change. If it isn't apparent at first glance, look again. There is one there. It is yourself.

Although at an advanced level of awareness we may ultimately be able to move mountains with our thoughts, most people find that there are some outside events that they cannot change. You can, however, change yourself or your attitude towards them. It's like stress. Stress is only what we perceive for ourselves to be stressful. For someone else the outside events that bother you could be highly enjoyable.

That's very easily said but just how do you set about doing it? Well, the first thing is not to give yourself a hard time about your addictions. Acknowledge them and give yourself a hearty pat on the back for recognising them in the first place, and for deciding to do something about them. That's the first step. Then move on. There are four ways of dealing with the things in your life you don't like and can't change. Consider the following and decide which you think is the best.

You can ignore them
You can bury them
You can learn to live with them
You can deal with them by changing your internal programming

Ignoring them will inevitably lead to mental distress and physical disease, and you will be living in a fantasy world. If you bury them, you will also suffer mental distress and physical disease and by bottling it up there is every chance of a major blow-out or sadness and frustration later in life. And if you learn to live with them, very often the strain will be too much and you will be forced to revert to burying them again. But, if you deal with them by changing your internal programming you will be rewarded with mental and physical ease.

So there cannot be much doubt as to which of these alternatives is preferable. The trick now is to be able to pinpoint your addictions. Each time you feel angry, sad, rejected, afraid or jealous, stop and think 'What is the real problem? What is it I really want?' You will find that you are never really upset for the reason you think you are. There is always some deeper underlying cause. Try it and see. Think of a time when you were angry or miserable or afraid. Work through that experience now and say to yourself 'I created the experience of...(be specific about the event) because I wanted...(be specific here too)'. Now ask yourself the following questions:

What did I really want?
What was bothering me most?
What would I most complain about in describing the situation to someone else?
What aspect of myself was reflected back to me?
What was I avoiding?
What was I not seeing?
What was I afraid of?
What was the threat?
What was the worst thing that could happen and what would have been the result if it had happened?
How would I like to have changed the situation?
What would have happened if it had been changed in that way?
What would it say about me if it had happened my way?
How did I want the people around me to be?
What do I have to do for them for it to be that way in future?
What would I do in the future?
How do I feel about myself now?

If you have answered these questions honestly you will undoubtedly have discovered by now that the reasons you were sad, mad or afraid were not in fact the same reasons as you originally thought. By delving deeply in this way you can get to the root cause of your feelings and thus sort out which are your preferences and which are your addictions.

If you are still experiencing difficulties, here is another method of addiction spotting which may work better for you. Close your eyes and imagine yourself to be in a cinema. Take the event you wish to consider and watch that event taking place before you on the screen. Now ask yourself, where is it happening? Who is involved? What is being said? Who is saying it? What emotions are they showing? Who is watching or listening? Has this happened before? If so, when? Look at the person on the screen playing yourself. How are they reacting? What are they saying? Does their response seem reasonable? If not, why not? How do you think it should change?

Now return to the present and relive the experience. As you do, pinpoint the addiction by asking the following questions:

I created the experience of. . .

Because I chose to addictively demand. . .
(List several answers if you need to and then choose the major one.)

My required outcome of this addiction is to feel. . .

Behind every addiction there is a required outcome. You must identify that outcome in positive terms. Make sure you can create and maintain it and remember that, until you learn to move mountains, the one thing you know for sure that you can control, change or maintain is yourself and the way you feel. So the saying is not I want to *be* intelligent or loving or patient or whatever it is you want. Rather it is I want to *feel* intelligent, loving, patient, and so on.

Let's take an example. You are the boss of a small business and one day you lose your temper with your secretary. You cannot find what you are looking for and you berate her for not having all your papers in order. Why did you lose your temper with her? Was it because she hadn't sorted out your papers? Probably not. The true reason, if you work through it would probably go more like this: 'I chose to be angry with my secretary for not having everything in order because I want to feel that the administrative work is taken care of so that I am free to get on with my own work'. What is the solution? Either streamline the administration or put on more staff! In other words, find an alternative and positive way to achieve the same goal.

It is truly amazing how many of us, already having 95 per cent of what we want, will spend 95 per cent of our time worrying about the other 5 per cent. Instead it would be a whole lot better if we were to concentrate on what works. Enjoy the 95 per cent you have and the other 5 per cent will eventually fall into line.

# CREATING FUTURE HEALTH

We've nearly come to the end of the journey into our-selves. All that's left to examine now is the future.

Being well is a mixture of a number of different things. It needs an awareness of the real significance of health, rather than a lackadaisical, happy-go-lucky, let's see what comes up today attitude towards your well-being. It also involves a willingness to be responsible for the decisions you take about your body and for the symptoms which are displayed. That's not to say that you are necessarily unwell when you have the symptoms of an illness. Indeed you may well decide that at that particular time and under those particular circumstances it is 'better' for you to re-tain some of those symptoms than to get rid of them completely. The important thing is that you recognise them for what they are and take responsibility for them.

It is always important to remember that all illness has a purpose. It serves you in exactly the way you designed it to, and if you succeed in getting rid of it before you are completely ready then you will have to develop another illness to replace it.

Take for example the case of George X. For most of his thirty-five years he was an alcoholic. Apart from often not being able to stand up very straight and viewing a good deal of life from a supine position, George managed to lead a fairly normal life and his general health was on the whole reasonably good. He rarely suffered from colds or the flu, and when everyone around him went down like flies with some epidemic or other he alone would stay standing, so to speak, joking that any germ foolish enough to try to invade his body would immediately be pickled in alcohol. Then, when his life eventually started to collapse around him, he took himself to Alcoholics Anonymous and gave up drinking. His life started to improve rapidly, except that he found that he was becoming prone to just about every disease going. He only had to be within coo-ee of a cold and he was in bed with a temperature like Vesuvius. In short, what George had done was to remove one illness and replace it with others. He wasn't ready to give up having some sort of illness so he merely substituted one for the other. He still needed something in his life, a crutch on which to lean in order to elicit sympathy from those around him. Illness also provided a chance to escape from time to time from the stresses of his life, particularly from his job where the pressure of everyone's expectation that he would rise in the ranks was often too much to bear.

Finally George was persuaded to rethink his life and take a closer look at his feelings. He began to understand how the old patterns had been formed and why he had compensated by drinking too much. He realised that once the drink had gone he had to have something to take its place. Above all, he realised why illness was necessary in his life and why he had created it for himself. He was now ready to thank his alcoholism for serving him so well for all those years and to acknowledge himself for being smart enough to realise that he needed something to cover up for the emotional turmoil and deprivation he had experienced as a child. His next step was to say to himself, 'It really is unimportant now whether any illness I fall prey to stays or goes. I no longer need an illness to lean on. I might as well dispense with being ill and be well instead. I can have my emotional needs met by being more open with my family, and particularly my wife.' In fact, when he and his wife talked about his work and he explained that he didn't really feel he could cope with the extra responsibility of a promotion, she was able to acknowledge that she too had been nervous about this and the extra entertaining it would have entailed.

From that day on George began to be well, although he still lets himself become ill on occasions because he knows that illness can serve a useful purpose in life. The difference now is that George understands the true nature of illness and is in charge of it rather than the other way around.

To emulate George you have to be prepared to take total responsibility for your health. Many people find this a frightening prospect because it means that you have to admit that any illness you may develop is of your own making. By curing yourself you might stop the flow of sympathy or attention your illness brought you, or you might not be able to manipulate certain people as successfully if you become well. It also means that you would now have to be responsible for that cure. Gone would be the days when you could nip round to your local doctor for a bit of a whinge and a load of pills and potions. Gone too would be the opportunity to complain vociferously to anyone who would listen about how rotten your doctor was because he never seemed to know what was wrong with you or how to cure you.

Another common fear which stops many people taking responsibility for their own health is the fear of digging up the deeper problems which underlie their lives. Most people intuitively realise that there is some emotional skeleton in their cupboard and most people tend to steer well clear of opening the cupboard door. However, if you are brave enough to learn the ways of teasing the spiders out of the closet, eventually you will be able to take full responsibility for yourself and feel jolly proud for doing so.

Sometimes it can be a great relief to be ill and have to surrender all responsibility to someone else. It can also be a shrewd way of getting what you want without actually being seen to ask for it. So the first thing to realise is that it takes considerable courage to take full responsibility for your own health, but if you are prepared to do so then the rewards are ultimately massive. People who are prepared to face this challenge tend to be successful, secure and contented with their lives. If the process is begun early enough in life by parents encouraging their children to take this responsibility for themselves, powerful children who are in control of their bodies will be created. It is likely that these children will then grow up to be healthy and successful adults.

As you have seen earlier in this book, the attitude of parents towards health matters can radically affect their children. Unless children are actively encouraged to take complete responsibility for their own health from the start, rather than blaming other people or outside events, then, more likely than not, they will grow up mirroring the sickness of their parents.

Before you rush in here with protestations of innocence and non-responsibility, remember what we have said before. From the time you are born and take your first good look around you, you realise that this is a large, and possibly frightening, world. You also realise that you can be emotionally hurt if you express needs and they are denied, or that someone may take advantage of you if you expose your emotional vulnerabilities; on the other hand you learn that if you become physically sick you will be taken care of. Let us stress again: *do not feel guilty*. You have simply found a safe way of getting your needs met. Well done!

When it comes to doctors, it is amazing how most people have been conditioned to surrender totally to them. The phrases we use reflect this state of affairs accurately — 'Doctor, I am in your hands', or 'I am under the care of my doctor at the moment'. If we are put into hospital we ask permission to leave, just as we ask permission if we want to stop a course of treatment. What is happening is that your subconscious instruction to the doctor is 'Please keep me safe. Confirm my illness and remove the pain, but leave me at least some of my sickness because I still need it.' If you have chosen your doctor well he may, at this stage, prescribe a course of pills for you. Perfect stuff! The pill confirms your illness, ensures its continued verification while at the same time eradicating the painful symptoms. Stop for a minute and think about anyone you know who is on permanent medication. See if you can analyse the true meaning of their sickness, but for heaven's sake don't rush off and tell them that they must throw away their pills and potions and stop seeing their doctor! For reasons which you are unlikely to understand they need their sickness and have a right to it. The question is, do you need yours?

Remember, too, that there is another side to this patient-practitioner coin. In much the same way as you need the doctor, the doctor also needs you. He needs to be needed or else he probably wouldn't have become a doctor in the first place. He has an emotional investment in retaining a steady supply of sick patients, and, if we are to be really cynical, it can be argued that to some degree he also has a financial investment in keeping you unwell. The great paradox of proper health care is that practi-

tioners should really be in the business of putting themselves out of business! How many do? It is a contract,
however, which has been developed through the ages and
is seen to be acceptable by all walks of society. The two
sets of needs, ours and the doctors, are mutually comple-
mentary and mutually supportive. The real truth of the
matter, however, is that left to its own devices the body
will more often than not heal itself, and modern medicine,
rather than curing you, has the effect of prolonging your
disease by treating the symptoms rather than the underlying physical and emotional cause solely in the interests
of someone's emotional needs. Worse than that, doctors
can actually cause new diseases and sicknesses in their
patients without actively meaning to do so. So much so, in
fact, that a name has been coined for these diseases, 'iatro-
genic' — diseases created by drugs or medical procedures.

To rid yourself of ill-health then, you have to take
complete responsibility, be prepared to take a few risks
and be totally honest with yourself. Are you prepared yet
to do that? After all, there are certain advantages to being
sick that you may not want to forgo just now. What are
those advantages? Well, for a start it's one way of avoiding
having to look closely at yourself. There is always the
sneaky suspicion that you may not quite like what you
find! Then there's the belief, fostered in childhood, that
you are safe when you are sick. After all, our society and
traditions dictate that you don't kick a man when he's
down! Sickness is also a good way for you to maintain your
belief system. For example, you may believe that the
world is a dangerous place to be, and that it is much safer
to be tucked up in bed. You may think that too much is
expected of you out there, and that it is much safer under
the covers. Alternatively, you may think that if you go
into the world as you are no-one will love you, but if you
are sick then you can elicit tons of sympathy. These are

just a few of the many beliefs that you can have about yourself, the world and other people, which can persuade you that sickness is a good thing.

So you see there are two quite distinct events occurring when you become sick. There is the physical manifestation, which, left to itself, will almost always cure itself, and the underlying emotional cause, which results in these physical symptoms, and which requires treatment of a kind before it will go away. The wise thing is not to deluge the body with drugs, thus creating other problems for yourself, nor should you set out to sabotage the treatment. Rather you should try to accept the responsibility for making yourself whole again by facing whatever emotional needs you have and whatever it is that has made you sick in the first place. On the part of practitioners, it would help if they realised that we, as patients, have a distorted view of ourselves. It would help if they began with the premise that we are, in fact, healthy people who have taken our illness upon ourselves. They could then assist us to see that we don't need to be ill anymore. The greatest role our doctors could possibly play would be in allowing us to face our fears and then in helping us to overcome them.

When all that is said and done we find ourselves back at that one vital word with which we started this book — *choice*. Through these chapters we have seen how our perceptions (conscious or not) of particular events and emotional triggers can affect our behaviour patterns. Our whole system of beliefs, and consequently our attitudes to life, have been constructed since our earliest days. Pre-birth conditioning and childhood patterning can, as we have seen, enormously influence our perceptions, although we are probably not even aware of it. We can choose to allow these perceptions to affect us badly — or we can ignore them altogether. In short, we often have a choice and through either conscious or subconscious means we exercise that choice, thereby determining our health patterns.

It should be stressed here that the choice you make is *not* always a rational, conscious one. Your conscious mind may well be saying 'The last thing I need at the moment is to go down with the flu', but your subconscious mind may well decide otherwise, believing itself to be the best judge of what is good for you. You can, however, learn to expose what has guided that choice and, having exposed it, examine it, deal with it as necessary — and become healthy.

Some of the ideas that we have put forward may seem somewhat difficult. If this is the case we ask you to consider that those ideas which cannot be *proved*, cannot, by the same token, be *disproved*. Faced with such a proposition the only way to deal with it, we suggest, is to accept the answer which is most *useful* to you at the time. Even the most unusual of the ideas we have propounded here work for thousands of people around the world, so why shouldn't they work for you?

In conclusion, we would say that your attitude towards your health is most probably a mirror of your attitude to life in general. You can either choose to be up and doing, or down and being done. Once again the choice is yours.

# REFERENCES

CHAPTER 4

1. Wambach, Dr Helen, *Life Before Life*, Bantam Books, New York, 1979
2. Purpura, Dr Dominick, 'Consciousness', *Behaviour Today*, 2 June 1975, p. 494
3. Wambach, Dr Helen, ibid., pp. 41, 42
4. Rottman, Dr Gerhard, 'Reading Maternal Stresses' in Untersuchungen uber Einstellung zur Schwangerschaft und zur fotalen Entwiklung, *Geist und Psyche*, Munich, 1974
5. Stott, Dr Dennis, 'Effects of Different Stresses, Follow-up Study from Birth of the Effects of Prenatal Stresses' in *Developmental Medicine and Child Neurology*, 15: 770–787, 1973
6. Spelt, D. K., Conditioned Learning in 'The Conditioning of the Human Foetus in Utero', *Journal of Experimental Psychology*, 38: 338–346, 1948
7. Verny, Dr Thomas, 'The Prenatal Self', *The Secret Life of the Unborn Child*, Sphere Books, London, 1982, p. 52

CHAPTER 5

1. Mendelsohn, Dr Robert S., 'How Doctors Manipulate Women', *Male Practice*, Contemporary Books, Chicago, 1981, pp. 17–18

CHAPTER 6

1. Harrison, Dr John, 'The Childhood Basis of Disease', *Love Your Disease*, Angus & Robertson, Sydney, 1984, p. 25

CHAPTER 8

1. Cheraskin, Dr Emanuel; Ringsdorf Jnr, Dr W. Marshall; and Sisley, Dr Emily L., 'Why C', *The Vitamin C Connection*, Harper & Row, New York, 1983, pp. 7–9

CHAPTER 9

1. Matthews-Simonton, Stephanie and Simonton, Dr Carl, 'The Search for the Causes of Cancer', *Getting Well Again*, Bantam Books, New York, 1980, p. 39

CHAPTER 10

1. Holmes, Dr T. H. and Rahe, Dr R. H., 'The Social Readjustment Rating Scale', *Journal of Psychosomatic Research*, 1967, 11: 213–218

CHAPTER 14

1. Orr, Leonard and Ray, Sondra, 'The Beginning', *Rebirthing in the New Age*, Celestial Arts, Berkeley, California, 1977
2. Orr, Leonard and Ray, Sondra, 'Hyperventilation', ibid., pp. 80–82

# FURTHER READING

Bach, Richard, *Jonathan Livingstone Seagull*, Pan Books, London, 1970

Berger, Dr Stuart, *What Your Doctor Didn't Learn in Medical School*, Bantam Books/Schwartz Publishing, Sydney, 1988

Biddulph, Steve and Biddulph, Shaaron, *The Making of Love*, Doubleday, Sydney, 1988

Capra, Fritjof, *The Turning Point*, Flamingo Books, London, 1982

Cousins, Norman, *Anatomy of an Illness*, Bantam Books, New York, 1981

Gawain, Shakti, *Creative Visualisation*, Bantam Books, New York, 1982

Harris, Dr Thomas A., *I'm OK — You're OK*, Pan Books, London, 1973

Harrison, Dr John, *Love Your Disease*, Angus & Robertson, Sydney, 1984

Hay, Louise, *You Can Heal Your Life*, Specialist Publications, Australia, 1984

Jampolsky, Dr Gerald, *Love is Letting Go of Fear*, Bantam Books, New York, 1981

Johnson, Robert A., *He*, Religious Publishing Company, Philadelphia, 1974

Johnson, Robert A., *She*, Religious Publishing Company, Philadelphia, 1976

Johnson, Robert A., *We*, Religious Publishing Company, Philadelphia, 1978

Keyes, Ken, *Taming Your Mind*, Living Love Publications, Oregon, 1975

Leonard, Jim and Laut, Phil, *Rebirthing: The Science of Enjoying All of Your Life*, Trinity Publications, Ohio, 1983

Matthews-Simonton, Stephanie; Simonton, Dr Carl; and Creighton, James L., *Getting Well Again*, Bantam Books, New York, 1980

Orr, Leonard and Ray, Sondra, *Rebirthing in the New Age*, Celestial Arts, Berkeley, 1977

Ray, Sondra and Mandel, Bob, *Birth and Relationships*, Celestial Arts, Berkeley, 1987

Verny, Dr Thomas with Kelly, John, *The Secret Life of the Unborn Child*, Sphere Books, London, 1981

Wambach, Dr Helen, *Life Before Life*, Bantam Books, New York, 1979

# INDEX

Acceptable illness, 77, 151-53
Acupuncture, 129
Addictions, 173-78 see also
    Needs
Alexander technique, 129
Allopathy, 130
Ambitions, 159-61, 170-72
Anger, 103-109
Aroma therapy, 130
Autonomic nervous system, 46

Bach flower therapy, 130
Belief in oneself, 81-82, 167
Bereavement, 116
Bio-feedback, 100-102
Bioenergetics, 130
Birth experiences, 55-58
Bloomfield, Dr A. L., 155
Body work, 130
Bonding, 58-59
Bone pointing ceremony,
    139-40
Breastfeeding, 85
Breathing technique for
    rebirthing, 142-43

Cancer, 116-17, 138-39
Caring for ourselves, 168-70
Carrel, Alexis Man,
    The Unknown, 19
Childhood conditioning, 67-79,
    165-67 see also Learning
Chiropractic, 130
Choice of lifestyle, 9-10,
    185-86
Choleric temperament, 14
Cleansing mechanism, 37-42
Conditioning in childhood,
    67-79, 165-67 see also
    Learning

Control over one's own life,
    22-24, 81, 158-61, 167-70
Creative visualisation, 28-33

Dental treatment, 121-22
Developmental stages, 13
Disease, 88-91 see also Illness

Einstein's theory of
    relativity, 18
Endorphins, 105
Energy, 18-20
Engrossment, 59

Faith-healing, 130, 133-34
Fasting, 130
Fate, 22-24
Fear, 103-109
Feldenkrais, 130
Foetus, 45-53

Gestalt, 130
Goals in life, 159-61, 170-72

Healing methods, 129-34
Herbalism, 131
Homoeopathy, 131
Hundredth Monkey Effect, 12
Hydropathy, 131
Hyperventilation, 142-43
Hypothalamus, 46, 97

Illness
    Acceptable, 77, 151-53
    caused by fear, 106-07
    caused by stress, 99-100
    Inherited, 150-51
    Using, 76-78, 179-85
    see also Disease
Immune system, 115-16, 117
Instinct and intuition, 82-83,
    91-93